DATE DUE

DEMCO 38-296

THE EUROPEAN UNION SERIES

General Editors: Neill Nugent, William E. Paterson, Vincent Wright

The European Union series is designed to provide an authoritative library on the European Union, ranging from general introductory texts to definitive assessments of key institutions and actors, policies and policy processes, and the role of member states.

Books in the series are written by leading scholars in their fields and reflect the most up-to-date research and debate. Particular attention is paid to accessibility and clear presentation for a wide audience of students, practitioners and interested general readers.

The series consists of four major strands:

- general textbooks
- the major institutions and actors
- the main areas of policy
- the member states and the Union

Published titles

Wyn Grant
The Common Agricultural Policy

Justin Greenwood
Representing Interests in the European Union

Fiona Hayes-Renshaw and Helen Wallace
The Council of Ministers

Simon Hix and Christopher Lord
Political Parties in the European Union

Brigid Laffan
The Finances of the European Union

Janne Haaland Matláry
Energy Policy in the European Union

Forthcoming

Simon Bulmer and Drew Scott
European Union: Economics, Policy and Politics

David Millar, Neill Nugent and William E. Paterson (eds)
The European Union Source Book

John Peterson and Elizabeth Bomberg
Decision-making in the European Union

Ben Rosamond
Theories of European Integration

Richard Sinnott
Understanding European Integration

• • • •

Simon Bulmer and Wolfgang Wessels
The European Council (Second Edition)

Renaud Dehousse
The Court of Justice: A Brief Introduction

David Earnshaw and David Judge
The European Parliament

Neill Nugent
The European Commission

Anne Stevens
The Administration of the European Union

• • • •

David Allen and Geoffrey Edwards
The External Economic Relations of the European Union

Michelle Cini and Lee McGowan
Competition Policy in the European Union

Martin Holland
The European Union and the Third World

Anand Menon
Defence Policy and the European Union

James Mitchell and Paul McAleavey
Regionalism and Regional Policy in the European Union

John Redmond, René Schwok and Lee Miles
Enlarging the European Union

Margaret Sharp and John Peterson
Technology Policy in the European Union

Hazel Smith
The Foreign Policy of the European Union

Mark Thatcher
The Politics of European High Technology

Rüdiger Wurzel
Environmental Policy in the European Union

• • • •

Simon Bulmer and William E. Paterson
Germany and the European Union

Phil Daniels and Ella Ritchie
Britain and the European Union

Alain Guyomarch, Howard Machin and Ella Ritchie
France in the European Union

Other titles planned include

European Union: A Brief Introduction
The History of the European Union
The European Union Reader
The Political Economy of the European Union

• • • •

Social Policy
Monetary Union
Political Union
The USA and the European Union

• • • •

The European Union and its Member States
Reshaping the States of the Union
Italy and the European Union
Spain and the European Union

Energy Policy in the European Union

Janne Haaland Matláry

St. Martin's Press
New York

ENERGY POLICY IN THE EUROPEAN UNION

St. Martin's Press, Scholarly and Reference Division,
175 Fifth Avenue, New York, N.Y. 10010

First published in the United States of America in 1997

This book is printed on paper suitable for recycling and
made from fully managed and sustained forest sources.

Printed in Hong Kong

ISBN 0–312–17295–8

Library of Congress Cataloging-in-Publication Data
Matláry, Janne Haaland.
Energy policy in the European Union / Janne Haaland Matláry.
p.   cm.
Includes bibliographical references and index.
ISBN 0–312–17295–8 (cloth)
1. Energy policy—European Union countries.   2. Energy industries–
–European Union countries.   3. Power resources—European Union
countries.   I. Title.
HD9502.E82M37   1997
333.79'094—dc21   96–47729
                                                            CIP

To Árpád, perennial critic

Contents

Acknowledgements   x

List of Abbreviations   xii

Introduction   1
Analytical approach   2
The setting for EU energy policy   6
The structure of this book   10

**1 The Development of Energy Policy in the
    European Union**   12
Introduction: the lack of an EU energy policy   12
The beginnings: the ECSC and Euratom   14
The turning point: the internal energy market   19
Extending the scope of energy policy   22
Conclusions   23

2 National Energy Policies in EU Countries   25
Introduction: the structural parameters   25
The producers: Netherlands, Denmark and Britain   28
The importers: Germany, France and Italy   32
The small importers: Austria, Belgium, Finland, Sweden
    and Luxembourg   40
The 'cohesion' countries: Ireland, Greece, Spain and
    Portugal   42
Conclusions   43

3 The Internal Energy Market   45
Introduction: the Commission as regulator   45
Deregulation and reregulation   46
A competence for networks   51
Policy on state aid   52
The IEM as a legal international regime   53
The Euro-Mediterranean strategy   54

Free market rules for exploration and production   55
Conclusions   56

4   Towards a Common Energy Policy?   **58**
Introduction: taking advantage of external 'windows of
    opportunity'   58
The CEP proposals   60
The fight for a formal competence   62
The environment and energy   65
Energy policy towards Central Europe and the CIS   71
Conclusions   77

**5   The Role of Member Governments and Interest
    Groups**   **79**
Governments and the internal energy market   79
Governments and the common energy policy   88
Domestic and EU-level strategies   93
The role of interest groups   95
Conclusions   103

6   The Role of EU Actors   **104**
The EU institutions and decision-making after the SEA
    and TEU   104
The Commission   106
The European Court of Justice and the Competition
    Directorate   119
The European Parliament   124
The Council of Energy Ministers   128
The European Council   129
Conclusions   130

**7   EU-Member States' Relations: Empirical
    Conclusions and Theoretical Implications**   **133**
Member governments and the energy policy-making
    process   133
The EU actors in the energy policy-making process   137
Theoretical implications: how to study the influence of
    non-state actors   141
Theoretical conclusions   149

Conclusion: The Future of EU Energy Policy   **151**

Guide to Further Reading   161

References   163

Index   172

Acknowledgements

The research for this study started in 1988/89 during a Fulbright research stay at the Foreign Policy Institute of the Johns Hopkins School of Advanced International Study in Washington, DC. There I was fortunate to work with Professor Wilfried Kohl and others with an interest in the political economy of energy trade. During that time I also benefited from discussions with scholars at the MIT and Cornell University, among them Richard Samuels and Peter Katzenstein.

At the Norwegian Institute of International Affairs (NUPI), where part of this study was written, I enjoyed the cooperation of Professor Martin Sæter, who, apart from being knowledgeable about energy, is an expert on EU integration. The study was completed at the Center for International Climate and Energy Policy Research (CICERO) of Oslo University. I wish to thank director Helga Hernes and Professor Arild Underdal for helpful comments and advice, and also for the generous amount of time off I was given from other research to complete this book in 1995. In my senior research position at ARENA (Advanced Research on the Europeanisation of the Nation-State), Oslo University, I was able to do the final revision of the manuscript.

The empirical material for the study was gathered over several years, starting in 1985, and included several rounds of interviews in the national capitals of the countries being studied and in the EU Commission in 1985, 1986, 1990 and 1992. I am grateful for the openness of the interviewees and respect their general wish to remain anonymous. Director Hans Maters of DGXVII was very helpful both in terms of substance and in providing me with contacts to discuss the work of the Commission.

Professor Stephen George, University of Sheffield, and Professor Walter Carlsnæs, Uppsala University, provided incisive criticism when my DPhil thesis on EU energy policy was defended in March 1994. Likewise I am indebted to Professors Knut Midgaard and Helge Hveem of the Institute of Political Science, Oslo University, for their helpful comments on the thesis, as well as to an anonymous reviewer who provided most helpful and detailed comments.

Two of our four children were born during the period of research for this study. They provided their mother with ample reminders of the relative importance of her academic undertaking. They, as well as my husband, luckily took no interest in the subject matter.

Oslo   JANNE HAALAND MATLÁRY

List of Abbreviations

bcm	billion cubic metres
CBI	Confederation of British Industry
CEDEC	European association of public sector energy distribution companies
CEEP	European public energy association
CEFIC	European chemical industry association
CEP	Common energy policy
CEPCEO	association of European coal producers
CERT	Committee on Energy, Research and Technology
CFM	Compagnie française de Méthane
CIPE	Interministerial Committee on Economic Planning
CIS	Confederation of Independent States
CSCE	Conference on Security and Cooperation in Europe
DREE	Direction des relations économiques extérieures
EBRD	European Bank for Reconstruction and Development
ECJ	European Court of Justice
ECSC	European Coal and Steel Community
EDC	European Defence Community
EEA	European Environmental Agency
EEC	European Economic Community
EiB	European Investment Bank
EMU	Economic and Monetary Union
ENI	Ente nazionale idrocarburi
EP	European Parliament
EPC	European Political Community
ETUC	European employees' association
EU	European Union
Euratom	European Atomic Energy Community
Europia	European oil producers' association
Foratom	European association of nuclear industry
IAEA	International Atomic Energy Agency
IEA	International Energy Agency
IEM	Internal Energy Market
IFIEC	European general industry association

IMF	International Monetary Fund
IPPC	Integrated Pollution Prevention and Control
IRI	Istituto riconstruzione industriale
MMC	Monopolies and Merger Commission
mtoe	million tons of oil equivalent
NEPP	National Environmental Policy Plan
Ofgas	Office of Gas Supply
OPEC	Organisation of Petroleum Exporting Countries
PHARE	Pologne-Hongrie: Assistance à la Réconstruction Économique
RECHAR	EU Coal restructuring programme
SAVE	Specific Actions for Vigorous Energy Efficiency
SEA	Single European Act
SNGSO	Société Nationale de Gaz de Sud-Ouest
TACIS	EU programme for upgrading nuclear sector in the CIS
TEU	Treaty on European Union
UNCED	United Nations Conference on Environment and Development
UNICE	European employers' association

Introduction

Energy policy in the European Union has never been one of the main areas of integration, and for this reason this policy area has attracted little scholarly attention among analysts of the EU, apart from those primarily interested in energy. However after 1985 period energy policy became one of the concerns of the general internal market programme giving rise to various initiatives of an integrative character designed and carried out by the Commission. Energy policy is also one of the fields in which there have been major and persistent conflicts of interests between the Commission, member governments, and interest groups. The role of member governments in this policy area has traditionally been dominant, and in many ways still is. The emergence of the EU as a major actor in European energy policy since 1985, however, has brought about a decisive shift in the importance of energy policy on the EU agenda compared with the preceding 85 period. A central concern of this book is to explain how and why this has happened and in particular how the Commission has become a major actor in energy policy, and what are the conditions for its ascendance and decline.

While the internal market programme boosted energy policy developments at the EU level, since 1992 there has been a general slowing down of Commission initiatives, as well as a much less expansionist agenda. The Commission may still be aiming to create a common energy policy with a formal mandate ('competence') for itself, but since about 1992 there has been little political scope for this. The momentum created by the internal market seems to have been lost.

This book primarily focuses on EU energy policy-making in the period 1985–95, and seeks to throw some light on why the Commission has such influence in an area where member governments have always been the key actors. The role of member governments is therefore the starting point of the analysis. Before 1985 few if any analysts accorded any role to the EU in energy policy-making. Thus in studying how and when the Commission gained influence in this policy area it is with this 'bottom line' in mind as any deviation from member governments as the main actors is both empirically and theoretically interesting.

What explains the gradual emergence of an EU energy policy? What explains the persistence of the EU agenda in terms of a common energy policy when member governments are so opposed to such a move? Are there advantages for member governments in creating (and therefore supporting) a certain measure of common EU energy policy, or is the latter happening *in spite of* the member governments? These are the questions posed in this book.

We will follow the development of EU energy policy from its beginnings in the European Coal and Steel Community (ECSC) and the European Atomic Energy Community (Euratom), to the internal energy market, launched in 1988 to the policy battles over the major Commission initiatives up to the eve of the intergovernmental conference in 1996, where energy policy is on the agenda as a possible new competence of the EU. The analysis contrasts the roles of the main member governments – France, Germany, Italy and Britain – with those of other actors such as interest groups, but mainly the Commission, the European Council, the Council of Ministers, the European Court of Justice (ECJ) and the European Parliament (EP). We will focus on the most controversial directives introduced under the heading of the internal energy market (IEM), and the proposals made between 1989 and 1992 for the creation of a common energy policy, where the role of EU actors would be greater than that of just market deregulator. By studying the negotiations over these various policy proposals and their outcomes we will be able to see how those taking part have cooperated and how proposals have been traded over, linked or rejected. We will also gain an insight into how the Commission works to advance its proposals, and how it has gained (and sometimes lost) influence.

Analytical approach

As indicated above, member governments are probably the most decisive actors in European and EU energy policy. Since this is a new area where the EU institutions enjoy no formal competence, we can safely assume that the member governments will remain at the forefront of the process. In this analysis we will therefore use a model that is often referred to as Putnam's 'two-level games' (Putnam, 1988). Strictly speaking this is a metaphor rather than a true model, but it may be a useful tool for understanding why member governments engage in EU-level policy-making.

Putnam argues that a government is able to 'play games' at both the domestic and at the international (here EU) level once it has gained access to the latter arena. For example, if a government is finding it difficult to gain acceptance for an unpopular policy at home, it may invoke international commitments such as binding EU rules. Likewise at the international level it may argue that domestic constraints make it unable to fulfil an international obligation. Like Ulysses, it is tied to the mast – willingly if it is autonomous enough to do the tying itself, or unwillingly if domestic groups 'tie it in'. It follows from this that a government that enjoys autonomy in a particular issue area, here energy, can play games at both levels, whereas one that is severely constrained by domestic interest groups cannot do so easily, although it can invoke international commitments to stave off domestic policy battles.

In the empirical analysis below we will apply this analytical framework to the interaction between member governments at the EU level, looking first for clues to government autonomy: which governments are in fact able to pursue their own strategies without hindrance?

To this end we also need to determine what government interests exist in energy policy. Putnam's model assumes rational and instrumental actor interests – that governments have interests that are discernible and determined *prior* to negotiations at the EU level. This is a problematic assumption that is currently much debated in the literature, but we choose it here for two reasons: (1) in energy policy it is likely that we will find such basic 'structural' interests, and (2) in the course of the analysis we will be able to see when this assumption does not hold. In other words, we may find that the interests are generated by the policy process itself.

According to Putnam a government is a gate-keeper between the domestic and the international levels. Here we must assume that the government is able to distinguish clearly between domestic and EU policy-making, and that information and policy activity takes place at both levels. We also have to assume that other actors do not approach the EU arena directly, for instance interest groups. Likewise member governments are assumed to be so dominant in the policy-making process that they can be certain of such control. These assumptions too are problematic, and at the end of the book we will discuss how valid they have been in terms of our analysis.

Putnam identifies four government strategies. An *offensive international* strategy can be pursued by a strong, or very autonomous, government: it will be successful in its bid to influence the outcome of international negotiations to its domestic advantage. A *defensive international* strategy will be selected by a weaker government: it will not be able to change the international rules, but will at least be able to invoke them at home. An *offensive domestic* strategy is used by a government that is able to shape policy at home but is not able to play games at both levels, and thus cannot exploit the possibilities inherent in this. A *defensive domestic* strategy is used by a government that is so weak that it has to conform to strong domestic pressure.

These strategies are narrowly defined and as such are rarely found in the real world. However they may be useful as classificatory devices that underline the differences between actors in terms of their ability to also use the second level of policy-making to their advantage. Applied to the EU, their usefulness lies in its helping us to understand basic political mechanisms at the domestic and the EU level. It is undoubtedly true that most governments try to use the second level by invoking EU rules, for instance in the political battles leading up to the proposed economic and monetary union (EMU). Government representatives may declare that their country is already tied to the mast, and justify this with the long-term advantage of lowering inflation and avoiding undue political pressure to expand the national budget.

Indeed the attraction of Putnam's model lies in its suggestion that this mechanism explains why governments accept EU-level policy-making and have even signed away political power to the EU in the treaties. They derive direct benefit from this by creating a second level or arena to which only they have access. But why is it that only governments can play this two-level game? The answer to this depends on domestic constraints and opportunities as well as on the role of other EU actors.

Putnam's framework does not address the role of non-state actors at the international level. The ECJ, the Commission and the EP are not assumed to be actors in the way that governments are. There is no room in this model for these actors – they are simply assumed away, and the second level is exclusively made up of government participants.

This assumption is widely shared by analysts of the EU, where the mainstream approach is the intergovernmental one, which assumes that 'governments are the fundamental actors, they act in an instrumental fashion, and therefore, the formation of preferences analytically precedes bargaining' (Moravcsik, 1995, p. 613). This is the central approach that in the 1970s replaced neofunctionalism, until then the dominant approach to EU studies. It is also the main analytical one in the study of international relations. For this reason alone it makes sense to adopt it here. Also, as there is no suitable alternative model it is important to determine the extent to which it can help explain the development of EU energy policy in this period.

Thus while the starting point remains an intergovernmental one, the intention here is to test how far this approach goes towards explaining the outcomes of the negotiations over energy policy. It assumes, and therefore also predicts, that governments' actions account for policy outcomes, thereby relegating no independent role to EU-level actors.

To sum up, according to this model the first hypothesis is that the *only significant actors are governments*. Furthermore it is assumed that their interests are formed prior to decision-making at the EU level, and are instrumental. Hence the second hypothesis: *all policy-making outcomes in the EU process can be traced to prior government interests*, mainly economic interests. The counterhypotheses to these are that institutional EU actors matter independently, that interests may be formed during the policy-making process itself and not prior to it, and that interests may be other than economic.

We do not think that either set of hypotheses captures the full reality of EU energy policy-making, and that the one derived from intergovernmental premises may be in need of serious modification. It is likely that EU-level actors matter independently in some types of policy-making, under some conditions, and in some phases of policy-making. There is already a growing body of literature on the importance of the Commission as an actor, which will be discussed in Chapter 7. Likewise there are studies that deal with the concept of interests and interest formation that indicate that the former are not generated in isolation at the domestic level, but in a process that involves both the EU and the domestic level; and that these interests are not necessarily instrumental, but may be of a more long-term, broadly political kind (Sandholz, 1993). Thus there is growing opposition to the use of the intergovernmental paradigm to help understand and explain EU-level policy-making (Wincott, 1995), but as yet is no alternative approach has evolved. The empirical evidence we possess needs to be compared and assessed systematically before such an approach can be constructed.

This study adds yet another case, that of energy policy, to this growing body of empirical knowledge. Once we have examined the evidence in terms of actor importance, interest formation and pursuit, and policy outcomes we will be able to return to the theoretical discussion in assessing the utility of the intergovernmental approach that underlies Putnam's model.

The setting for EU energy policy

Since 1985 the agenda of the EU has grown to include a variety of policy areas. The Single European Act (SEA) marked a turning point in EU policy. Its introduction of qualified majority voting for internal market proposals in the Council of Ministers meant that decision-making was speeded up, and no member state wished to be seen as a laggard in the policy-making process. The institutional dynamics of the SEA and the internal market project together account for much of the dynamism of EU-level policy-making in the post-1985 period.

However external events have prompted much of the increased activity in the EU and the extension of its agenda to include energy policy. The demise of the former Soviet Union and the opening up of Central Europe brought new issues onto the EU agenda. In the energy field this meant that the EU suddenly had to coordinate and formulate policy to deal with this region and with the restructuring of its energy sector. In addition the increasing importance of environmental policy in Europe meant that the question of how to integrate environmental criteria into other policy-making, notably that involving the energy sector, received sustained attention. This need was underlined by the widespread dirtiness and wastefulness of energy use in the central part of Europe, and by the many unsafe nuclear installations in the CIS.

Thus in the 1990s the EU's energy agenda has consisted of a variety of policy items that relate to deregulation, the environment, security of supply and the region of Central Europe. This agenda was formed in the span of a few years and without any explicit legal basis for developing a comprehensive energy policy. There is still no formal competence for this policy area in the EU.

Deregulation

Most energy policy in Europe is still made at the level of the member state. By its very nature energy policy is part of both economic policy and security policy, and increasingly also of environmental policy. In the economic area there is a clear development towards market deregulation and liberalisation in most European countries. The gas, coal and electricity sectors have traditionally been characterised by state monopolisation of production, transmission and distribution, reflecting the postwar European concern with security of supply and the need to protect domestic energy sources. Energy in this sense has always been a security policy issue of the highest order.

Since the 1980s, however, there has been a process of deregulation of the energy sector in Europe, especially in Britain. The internal market concept of the EU was born in this general political climate. One may thus say that whereas energy policy was formerly a national concern, with national supply foremost on the agenda, today there is an evolution towards more market-based thinking where national borders are not so important. This line of development underlies the internal market philosophy, but in the energy sector there are still many obstacles to this way of thinking as a general paradigm for energy policy. Many energy sector executives argue that energy production, transmission and distribution are 'natural monopolies' and that supply is a public service function. As we shall see, whether the energy sector should be treated as a market governed by commercial rules or as a sector to be managed by public firms lies at the heart of the political controversies over the internal energy market.

There are still several member countries where the state is the monopoly owner of or at least retains a major presence in the energy companies. While deregulation has been carried almost to its limit in Britain, it is only just beginning in France and Italy. In Germany there is a mixture of state policy in the coal and nuclear sector and a free market approach in other parts of the energy sector.

Although the trend towards deregulation is favoured as a move that will lead to lower energy prices, there are major differences between countries where deregulation is being attempted or implemented, and those where this is not the case. The prospects for a common energy policy in the EU are therefore not very good. While there exists a shared interest in some aspects of a common policy, there is likely to be strong resistance to an increase in the roles of EU institutions in this policy area.

A further controversy between member governments concerns what deregulation entails in terms of political control. Here the recent British practice of sharply separating the market from politics, of 'rolling back the state' as Thatcher expressed it, contrasts strongly with the continental preference for *dirigisme*. This difference in policy styles is also important in other policy areas, for example environmental policy (Heritier *et al.*, 1994).

A deregulated market needs rules, as well as institutions to ensure that the rules are being adhered to. Thus a logical role for the Commission is that of regulator. This may turn out to be a politically powerful position: Majone has described the new tasks of the state in Europe – and by implication those of the Commission – as overseeing and managing regulation: 'Privatisation and deregulation have created the conditions for the rise of the regulatory state to replace the *dirigiste* state of the past. Reliance on regulation rather than public ownership, planning or centralised administration characterises the method of the regulatory state' (Majone, 1994, p. 1). This phenomenon is a general one that has been observable in Europe since about 1980: 'in Europe, the terms "deregulation" and "privatisation" gained sudden currency – even in Great Britain the words were scarcely heard before 1978' (ibid., p. 2).

It is within this general context of change that the internal energy market is taking shape, and the terms of this debate are therefore central to both the Commission's arguments and those of the various interest groups in the sector, some of which want to deregulate the sector while others take the opposite view. The role of the deregulator may thus be politically very important, both because this will be a role of increasing importance, and because the Commission may seek to utilise it as a power base.

Security of supply

Although there has been a marked emphasis on deregulation in the energy policies of many member states, on the whole the role of national governments has remained strong. This is typical of a sector where security of supply is an ever present concern, since most EU countries are heavily dependent on imported fuel. Oil continues to account for a large proportion of the energy consumption of all modern economies, and this fuel type will become even more important with the expansion of the transport sector in the so-called 'cohesion' countries – the less developed EU members. Oil is sold on the world market, but the bulk of supplies will continue to come from non-European countries. Security of supply will therefore remain an important political issue for individual countries as well as for the EU as a whole. In a Green Paper on a common energy policy, published by the Commission in early 1995, ensuring security of supply was presented as one of the main problems in the energy field in the years ahead, along with the environment and the continued work on the internal energy market (IEM), and in the White Paper that followed it, security of supply was one of the main goals of EU energy policy.

The environment

Another issue that will remain on the political agenda is the environment, despite the slow pace of policy-making in this area. Not only CO_2 emissions, but other sorts of air pollutants that result from the extraction and consumption of fossil fuels will be in focus. The burning of coal leads to the release of large amounts of CO_2 and SO_2 into the atmosphere. Oil is a little more 'benign' and natural gas is considered the cleanest of the fossil fuels. While nuclear energy has none of the drawbacks of coal, its continued use is very controversial because of the question of safety during production and waste storage.

The 'added dimension' of the environment has made energy policy much more complicated than before: policy-makers not only have to take continued supply into account, they also have to consider the environmental implications of each fuel type. Increasingly governments have had their hands tied in terms of international environmental obligations that set limits for emissions of various kinds. These international commitments must be met domestically, and thus coordination of energy and environmental policies is increasingly required at the national level. Global warming is the latest and most complicated of these issues.

The EU is a signatory to international environmental agreements and is developing the environmental dimension of energy policy in order to comply with them. So far, however, this work has not been very successful. Some EU countries have made great advances in integrating environmental criteria into energy policy – the Netherlands and Denmark stand out in this respect. Others still face large environmental problems, and the hope of the latter group of countries is that common policies at the EU level will play a large part in resolving these problems.

The structure of this book

In the following chapters we will analyse the development of EU energy policy with special emphasis on the post-1985 period. In Chapter 1 we recount the history of EU energy policy from the beginnings of the ECSC and Euratom in order to provide a background to more recent EU energy policy.

The trend towards deregulation, as stated is, a fairly recent one in Europe, where the energy sector has been characterised by state monopolisation. Energy policy has traditionally been considered a national concern, so an analysis of individual energy policies is provided in Chapter 2.

In Chapters 3 and 4 we present an in-depth analysis of the EU energy policy proposals and their implications. Chapter 3 deals with the internal energy market including the difficult issues of 'third party access' to gas and electricity transmission, price transparency and competition in public procurement. The general role of the internal market mandate is analysed in terms of its importance to the internal energy market, as is the importance of competition legislation in prising open monopolistic energy sectors. The relationship between the Competition Directorate and the European Court of Justice (ECJ) is of special relevance here. Since 1990, competition legislation has been increasingly applied to the energy sector, which previously had been left untouched.

Chapter 4 analyses the Commission's attempt to bring about a common energy policy, the proposals for which include a formal competence for such a policy being laid down in the treaties. So far nothing has come of this, but it remains on the agenda. The Commission's agenda for energy policy includes additional formal powers for itself: It has tried to develop a pan-European energy strategy for Central Europe and the CIS as well as an energy policy that takes environmental concerns into account. Both types of policy need some sort of centralised policy-making capacity and are not based on the deregulation of energy markets.

In Chapters 5 and 6 the process of EU energy policy-making is analysed. Here we are interested in the relative roles of the various actors – member states, interest groups and EU institutions. Chapter 5 analyses the role of the major member states – Germany, Britain, France and Italy – as well as that of the energy industry and other interest groups in EU energy policy. Chapter 6 does the same for the various EU institutions.

In Chapter 7 the relative roles of these actors is compared and evaluated, and we discuss what the findings imply for integration theory and how we conceptualise integration in general. In the Conclusion we discuss the likely outcome of EU energy policy in the years ahead.

1

The Development of Energy Policy in the European Union

Introduction: the lack of an EU energy policy

Energy policy, in Europe as elsewhere, has traditionally been a national concern. Countries are endowed differently in terms of energy resources, and have different import needs and consumption patterns. Among the countries of this study, Britain is nearly self-sufficient in both oil and gas, whereas Italy imports close to 80 per cent of its energy. Because of these differences there has not been a major rationale to develop an energy policy at the EU level. Also, member states have been opposed to an EU-wide energy policy.

However the 'oil shock' of 1973–74 led to multilateral cooperation and the creation of the International Energy Agency (IEA), which aimed to erect a buffer against price hikes and introduce an emergency oil-sharing mechanism (Toner, 1987). In what was then the EC there was also concern about dependence on imported oil, but 1988 energy policy did not really develop beyond recommendations in the form of guidelines that were not binding on the member governments. Energy was conspicuously absent from the general competences of the EC but there was nonetheless a gradual development towards such a policy.

Looking at the directives on energy in the period 1973–88 it is clear that much attention was devoted to security of supply, research and conservation. In the 1970s EC directives dealt with how to handle supply interruptions and how to coordinate investment in and

12

import/export of oil and gas, and under the ECSC and Euratom a series of regulations were issued that dealt with various aspects of trade in these energy forms. After 1985 there was a large surge in EC legislative output, although there was no single vision of the form to be taken by EC energy policy.

Not surprisingly, therefore, the conventional academic view has been that energy policy is one of the 'weakest' policy areas of the EC/EU. George (1991) concludes that energy policy may develop beyond national policies in the 1990s, but that it remains an area where national policies are very strong indeed. Padgett (1992) finds that 'the strategic economic importance of the energy sector meant that policy autonomy was guarded jealously by national governments'. At the time of these studies the internal energy market (IEM) was already under way.

This book modifies the conclusion that energy is a weak area in EU policy-making and shows that it has been moving towards increased integration in some areas from the inception of the IEM to the present. This development, however, has been very uneven as member governments have halted the process in major areas but supported it in others. There is still no formal common energy policy (CEP), nor is there an official mechanism to develop one.

This chapter traces the development of EU energy policy from its beginnings to the present. After discussing the two founding treaties designed to deal with questions of energy – the ECSC and Euratom – we move to the inception of the internal market in 1985. We will show how EU energy policy has moved from one based on common guidelines and unanimous decision-making, to the IEM, and now towards a CEP; arguing that elements of a CEP began to materialise from about 1990 onwards, along with intensification of the process towards the IEM. This development, it is argued, represents one of *integration* in the energy policy area.

Integration in energy policy is conceived of here as an *intended* effect of policy development. The ability of the Commission both to define policy and to forge links between formal and informal policy areas allows it to design policies in such a way that its own institutional role is enhanced. An example of formal integration in this area is the linking of energy and environmental policies, whereby the Commission would acquire an implicit mandate to develop policy in areas dealing with the encouragement of environmentally friendly sources of energy. As we shall see, this is a very different type of policy issue than those that derive from the IEM. Likewise an example of formal integration in energy policy would be the Commission being assigned the task of developing the energy infrastructure of the EU region and beyond as part of the general competence for networks defined in the Treaty on European Union.

In sum, although the lack of a formal mandate to develop energy policy at the EU level continues to hamper the Commission's work in this area, its agenda continues to contain CEP proposals because unexpected external events make an international-level response logical, at least in some cases. The role of the Commission has been important in some stages of decision-making – more in agenda-setting than in final negotiations – and it has been more important in some energy policy areas than others, notably in the areas where member states have not yet developed their own policies. This book focuses on these role differences in an attempt to highlight the conditions for EU influence. As such, it seeks to add empirical knowledge of one issue area to the accumulated studies of EU policies in the post-1985 period.

The beginnings: the ECSC and Euratom

Energy policy in the EC/EU has traditionally been rather insignificant despite the paradox that two of the three original treaties, the ECSC and Euratom, both concerned energy. The European Coal and Steel Community (ECSC), which was established by the Treaty of Paris, came into existence in 1952 and created a *de jure* common market in coal. The treaty mandated the ECSC to establish guidelines for coal policy in a way that would contribute to 'economic expansion, growth of employment and a rising standard of living'. The signatories 'shall place financial resources at the disposal of undertakings for their investment and shall bear part of the cost of readaptation' (Article 2). The treaty expressly forbade all types of state aid, but in reality this has meant little.

The architect of the treaties, Jean Monnet, had conceived of a coal and steel union in the belief that cooperation between France and Germany would lead to lasting peace in Europe (Griffiths, 1996, p. 28). After the Second World War Europe needed energy for general reconstruction, and coal made up about 80 per cent of primary energy use at that time. There was a shortage of coal, which was alleviated by American imports, facilitated by the terms of Marshall Aid. But in Europe the steel industry also relied on German coal, and it therefore seemed an excellent idea to try to forge integration between the two old foes – France and Germany – by creating a common policy for coal and steel production. This was an instrument to advance peace building; a functional tool of economic policy that would lead to lasting peace, it was hoped. The French foreign minister, Robert Schuman, declared in a speech on 9 May 1950 that this was 'concrete, resolute action on a limited but decisive point' (Archer, 1994, p. 75). Since coal was the predominant energy source in Europe and the main input to steel production, the ECSC seemed a brilliant concept. The precursor of the treaty, the so-called Schuman Plan, proposed to place all German coal and French steel production under a supranational authority, the so-called High Authority, but the Treaty of Paris broadened its scope to include the Benelux countries and Italy.

As stated in the preamble to the treaty, the signatories would 'substitute for historic rivalries the merger of their essential interests [and lay] the foundations of a broader and deeper community among peoples long divided by bloody conflicts'. However the High Authority of the ECSC, which formally had clear supranational powers, did not become *dirigiste* in its orientation. On the contrary it confined its activity to promoting coal trade according to free market principles. When mild winters led to a coal surplus throughout Europe in 1958–59 the High Authority attempted to enforce a free market by acting against Germany and France, which instituted import barriers to protect domestic coal. The High Authority's action took the form of a request for emergency powers to prevent a complete standstill in the development of the common market in general, but this proposal did not achieve the majority agreement needed. Likewise, when coal subsidies were on the agenda some years later, the member states refused to agree to a system of joint financing. Monnet resigned in 1955 in disappointment at the failure of the ECSC to create a common energy policy (George, 1991).

In his detailed study of the creation and functioning of the ECSC, Milward concludes that 'The High Authority was but a powerful international committee within which separate national representatives urged for separate national policies' (Milward, 1992, p. 117). The intention had been otherwise – the High Authority was to have been indifferent to national interests and would act in the community's interest. The other institutions that were created, the Assembly and the Court, would supervise the work of the High Authority and render impartial judgements. The Council of Ministers, a late addition to the institutions, was conceived as a 'link' to national interests, but would not dominate decision-making. But the actual problems in the coal and steel markets were instead resolved by national and market actors. The coal surplus that gradually replaced the immediate postwar demand continued to expand, and European coal production became a problem because of this. The main question was how to restructure the coal sector and prevent dumping. Further, from around 1955 the share of coal in energy use fell drastically – the advent of cheap Middle Eastern oil triumphed in the market in the span of just a few years. By 1969 oil had become the dominant fuel (Clark, 1990).

As stated, the initial intention behind the ECSC had been a political one – the creation of peace – as Milward also concedes in his otherwise sceptical view of the role of political motives and ideas (Milward, 1992, p. 83). In terms of energy policy however, the ECSC did not lead to the development of a common energy policy covering energy sources other than coal. The focus of the ECSC was on how to manage coal and steel production in Europe in both its political and its economic implications, and not on creating a comprehensive energy policy.

Euratom was conceived to ensure there was enough energy to form a stable basis for economic growth and also to allow for the development of a European nuclear sector. Again the plan was that integration in the energy field would lead to further political integration, and again Monnet was instrumental in this endeavour.

After the ECSC several plans for sectoral integration were mooted: a 'green pool' for agriculture, a 'white pool' for health policy, a transport policy authority, a common defence policy in the form of a European Defence Community (EDC) and a European Political Community (EPC) (Archer, 1994). The thinking behind this was that sectoral economic integration would gradually lead to full economic and political integration with a federal system as the end result. However both the EPC and the EDC failed, and nothing came of the idea of sectoral integration in health and transport. However a common agricultural policy (CAP) was made part of the EEC in 1957.

At the time of the creation of Euratom, also in 1957, the importance that oil would assume in the industrialised world was not yet fully appreciated. The role of Euratom was thus that of creating the conditions 'necessary for the development of a powerful nuclear industry which will provide extensive energy resources' (Preamble,

Euratom Treaty). France took a special interest in the treaty as it was already the leading member state in terms of nuclear research, and hence stood to gain financially from EEC research funds. Germany was not enthusiastic about Euratom, but needed French support for the common market in general.

Deubner has provided a detailed account of the negotiations leading to the signing of Euratom. France was uninterested in developing the EEC – a general common market – and preferred the sectoral integration of various economic areas (Deubner, 1979). France proposed the founding of Euratom in 1955 to create, among other things, a common European nuclear market, a supply mechanism for uranium and a European enrichment plant. However the United States could supply uranium more cheaply and offered to do so to Germany. This led to the conclusion of a treaty that contained no strong measures to create a common European nuclear sector. Deubner dubs Euratom 'a "stillborn" integration scheme' (ibid., p. 223). The United States became the key supplier of enriched uranium and France developed a national nuclear sector. As George put it, 'even if the compromises written into the treaty were not enough, the first years of Euratom s life were sufficient to kill it in themselves' (George, 1991, p. 121).

Although Euratom began to fund joint research programmes, both Italy and Germany had already started their own nationally funded programmes in order to prevent France from continuing to dominate this sector. These countries also wanted to procure reactors built in the United States, something that was unpopular with the French.

A further hindrance to the development of common energy policy was the fact that the ECSC pressed for the promotion of coal in opposition to the nuclear lobby surrounding the Euratom bureaucracy. In this battle few political actors in the EC sensed that oil was on the rise as the dominant source of energy in Europe, and when Britain became an oil producer in the 1970s the case for individual national energy policies was entrenched. The oil crisis of 1973/74 saw EC countries opting for bilateral agreements with the Arab oil producers, who rewarded them according to their stance on the Arab–Israeli question. OPEC's (Organization of Petroleum Exporting Countries) *divide et impera* strategy worked brilliantly among the EC membership, and it was only because of an initiative by US Secretary of State Henry Kissinger (the founding of the International Energy Agency – IEA) that a common front was established in the form of cooperation on an emergency oil-sharing mechanism among most of the West European countries. But France again chose an independent strategy, and thus further delayed the possibility of a common energy initiative in the EC.

Thus, the High Authority of the ECSC was not given the supranational role envisaged in the Treaty of Paris, and in 1967 the three treaties and their institutions were merged. The situation in the 1960s and 1970s was one of eclecticism in terms of EC energy policy: oil had become the most important fuel, but the formal competences of the EC in energy policy concerned only coal and nuclear energy, both of which were diminishing in importance. Institutionally, 'with competences split among the treaties and other community acts, there are difficulties in achieving a common energy policy without institutional contradictions and ambiguities' (George, 1991, p. 184).

Analysing EC directives, regulations and guidelines from this period, one finds all the elements of 1985–95 energy policy: security of supply, coordination of investments and information on energy plans, attempts to introduce environmental measures in energy policy, as well as several measures relating to coal pricing, imports and production. The Commission tried to establish an internal energy market as part of the common market in 1968, but failed.

After 1973 the concern for security of supply loomed large in the directives, with the creation of 90-day emergency oil stocks in each member state, although, this was already in place in the IEA countries. Several directives dealt with other aspects of safeguarding the oil supply, but they only sought to coordinate national policies. There was no role for the Commission beyond this (Black, 1977).

Both the ECSC and the Euratom treaties have been rendered rather obsolete, since the ascendance of oil and gas as the dominant energy sources. The ECSC expires in 2002 and its fate beyond that date is uncertain. There has been some pressure to integrate the ECSC and Euratom in a chapter on a common energy policy in the new treaty to be negotiated at the intergovernmental conference in 1996–97, but there is little support for this on the part of member governments. The task confronting the coal sector in Europe in the 1980s and 1990s is that of restructuring and reducing production. Nuclear energy, on the other hand, remains important in the EU and may receive a boost from the twin concerns of import dependency on and the environmental problems caused by oil.

As it is based on the 'lowest common denominator' among member states with widely differing interests, EU energy policy has not amounted to much. Expressed in 'guidelines', it has been confined to suggestions to member governments on energy conservation, import dependency, research on renewable sources and so on. These guidelines, which are usually valid for a five-year period, represent a compromise between national energy policies.

The turning point: the internal energy market

The original intention of the Treaty of Rome was to create a customs union and, gradually, a barrier-free market. The concept of an internal market is thus not new to the EU, but was given a renewed emphasis in the process that started in 1985. At that time extreme pessimism reigned, and the oft-cited 'Eurosclerosis' was indicative of a certain economic gloom and inefficiency. The impetus for change came from growing concern about competition from Japan and the United States, as well as from within the EC itself.

The internal need for change must not be underestimated. In the EC in the mid 1980s there was considerable frustration and political elites and business leaders, especially in France and Germany, were discontented with the way the Community was developing, or perhaps with the lack of development. The effort to create an internal market was born of economic necessity and was largely designed by economic elites (Cowles, 1995), but it was carried out by political elites, particularly in France and Germany (Sandholz and Zysman, 1989). This was made possible by a new and generally accepted political attitude emphasising deregulation in order to achieve efficiently functioning markets. This new political trend gained support at the national level, not only in Tory Britain, but also in Mitterrand's socialist France. This laid the political basis for the launching of the EU internal market. The central argument – to which few objected on political or ideological grounds – was that a more efficient market would create growth and minimise costs (Padoa-Schioppa, 1987). There was a shared understanding of the economic problems as well as an ideological vision of the political 'cure'.

The Single European Act (SEA), adopted in 1986, brought changes to the decision-making procedure of the Community in order to facilitate the adoption of the 300 or so directives necessary for the creation of the internal market, as outlined in the White Paper on the Internal Market (EC, 1985). The introduction of qualified majority voting on the matters affecting the internal market meant that the EC could now adopt measures that were subject to a certain degree of disagreement – previously the need for unanimity had led to the collapse of many proposals. The adoption of the SEA was a major step in the process of formal integration. It transferred decision-making power to the institutions of the EC, primarily the Council of Ministers because the member states had relinquished their right to veto decisions. Furthermore the European Parliament (EP) was now able to play a more active role in amending proposals from the Commission (Meerhaege, 1989).

Thus the changes made in the SEA allowed the Commission greater independence and also accorded a large role to the EP. The Commission and the EP now had a mutual advantage in forming an alliance, as in combination they could see a proposal through the Council of Ministers unless the latter rejected it unanimously. The Treaty on European Union (TEU) from 1992 introduced further extensions of both the role of the EP and the use of majority voting in the Council.

Energy was not included in the White Paper but the concept of the internal market presented those in the energy field with a major challenge. In an internal energy market there must be competition and transparency, the Commission suggested. National energy monopolies faced dismantlement and national energy policies should follow suit to prise open energy markets. Thus the task of the Commission was a bold one indeed, since the European energy markets were considered to be among the most difficult to change, traditionally characterised by a heavy government hand in the form of strong national energy policies. This was the reason why energy was at first omitted from the internal market concept, only to be added as late as 1988 (EU, 1988a). It was, however, realised that the internal market would not be complete without a freer energy market; thus – more or less of necessity – energy was included in the general internal market process. Energy consumers were eager for lower prices, and as most member countries were and still are net importers of energy the IEM was an attractive concept for them. However in these states there were also monopolistic entities that were opposed to an IEM, and for a variety of reasons not all energy forms are suited for such competition.

Work on developing an IEM started in 1988. The first stage was made up of a package of directives, notably open access to gas and electricity supply, which is discussed in detail in Chapter 3. The opposition to this was formidable, particularly in the energy industry. The Council returned the most controversial directive, on gas transit, to the Commission at its meeting in May 1990. The directive was adopted in October 1991 by a majority vote. The second stage of the IEM consisted of a draft directive on the further opening up of the gas and electricity grids, presented in the form of two draft communications in late 1991 and later merged into one directive. The main concept here was that of third-party access, which would further open up the grids and allow third parties, that is sellers and buyers, to demand transmission of their energy against a given tariff. The proposal met very heavy resistance and still had not been adopted by the end of 1996.

The development of the IEM thus started with a package of four directives in 1989, proceeded with a restatement of the contents of these proposals in 1991, and extended the IEM beyond the EC area in the European Energy Charter the same year. The latter established a free-market regime for energy trade, discussed in detail in Chapter 4. The charter represents an extension of the IEM principles to the CIS (Commonwealth of Independent States), Central Europe and most of the Western world, and other significant aspects of the charter form part of a common energy policy. Furthermore, legislation on competition was increasingly applied to monopoly practises in the energy sector, and there were attempts to integrate environmental concerns into the IEM, for example a carbon tax and criteria for loans and financial aid to the energy sector in Central Europe.

From 1988–95 work on developing an IEM continued, despite widespread opposition from energy-sector interests and even governments. Although the member governments supported the idea of an IEM, they had strong reservations about the parts of it that directly affected their domestic energy sectors. In other words they supported the general concept, seeing that it might bring advantages to energy trade, but were wary of losing national control over energy policy.

Despite their deregulatory content the IEM proposals implied an increased role for the EC in energy policy: Firstly, third-party access and even the 'weaker' open access decision in 1990 implied that the Commission would oversee and define the conditions and tariffs for such access. This would require more centralised power in a new deregulatory agency within the EC or the Commission itself. Secondly, the Commission controlled some of the financing of energy developments in the less advanced economies of the Community. This eventually resulted in a new competence being included in the TEU for the development of infrastructure, the so-called trans-European networks. Thirdly, the Commission intensified its application of the rules on competition from about 1990 onwards by attacking not only the practise of monopoly but also the very existence of monopoly companies in the energy sector. It also began to intervene much more forcefully in national coal subsidy schemes. Fourthly, the Commission came to be perceived by interest groups as the major energy policy-maker in the European scene. The energy industry increasingly formed European-wide interest groups whose sole task was to lobby the EC, and the Commission's ability to incorporate these groups into the formal and informal negotiating system meant that it increased its own role as a negotiating partner and received expert knowledge as input to the political process.

Extending the scope of energy policy

From 1988 onwards EC energy policy developed markedly both as an integral part of the internal market and beyond. By the time of the launch of the IEM in 1988, general integration had taken place formally with the adoption of the Single European Act, and informally in the energy sector as a whole as energy policy increasingly came to include transnational issues such as energy shortages, the environmental problems in Central Europe, the environment in general, and so on. The scope of EC energy policy was thus continually being extended beyond the deregulatory nature of the IEM – policies. In this process of agenda building, defined as the linking of energy to other issues, the Commission was also the agenda setter, defining how this was to be done and consequently enhancing its powers as an international actor in energy policy. A by-product of this agenda building would be increased informal integration, as discussed in Chapter 4.

Thus EC policy-making on energy increased rapidly in the late 1980s. As a senior official of the Energy Directorate put it, 'energy is involved in a growing number of issue areas of the EC now' (Interview, Brussels, 1992).

External events seemed to be the precondition for much of this development: the Gulf War prompted EC policy proposals for IEA membership, an oil-sharing mechanism in the Community and EC interventions aimed at stabilising the price of oil. The energy supply problems in the CIS and Central Europe gave rise to the idea of the energy charter, and the international nature of environmental problems made energy a more pressing item on the EC agenda and its merging with energy policy a natural consequence. Furthermore internal reform facilitated the process of agenda building around energy policy. The procedural changes contained in the Single European Act made decision-making more efficient and removed the possibility of proposals being blocked by a single member state. Thus both national and interest group opposition could in some cases be overcome. All this may explain why there has been progress towards a common energy policy and an internal energy market, though albeit very slow progress, when so many important interest groups in the energy industry have opposed the concept.

At the end of 1995 a 'status report' on EU integration in energy policy included the following 'formal competences': the development of infrastructure in the EU region, especially in the less developed nations, and also beyond the EU region into Central Europe and across the Mediterranean; the granting of aid for the general development of the energy sectors in this region; the restructuring of aid to coal production in line with general EU state aid policy and the ECSC rules; the merging of energy and environmental policy as mandated in the Treatment on Political Union; intervention in national energy sectors to prevent monopolistic practises, and the continued existence of energy monopolies, based on the common policy on competition; and acting on behalf of the EU in the International Energy Agency and the United Nations Conference on Environment and Development (UNCED).

Informal policy-making roles have included establishing and administering control over some aspects of the transmission of gas and electricity, as well as setting the tariffs for such transportation; and implementing, managing and ensuring adherence to the rules of the charter until the end of 1995, when a separate charter organisation was established. Through this and other policy instruments, the EU has a major actor in the restructuring of the energy sectors of Central Europe and the CIS.

These developments are all the more significant because, as indicated in the Introduction, energy policy has been as a relatively uninteresting area in the study of EU integration.

Conclusions

Energy policy in the EC was prominent in two of the three founding treaties – the ECSC and Euratom – but it failed to lead to the development of a common energy policy. Member states had very different interests in the various forms of energy – France wanted to develop its nuclear sector, Germany had vast coal reserves and needed to support its coal industry – and the High Authority of the ECSE never became truly supranational. When oil became dominant in Western economies, dependence on Middle Eastern oil resulted in bilateral agreements between exporters and importers rather than in a common import policy. The launching of the EC internal market in 1985, however, spurred an effort to develop an internal energy market, and beyond that a common energy policy. This coincided with general support for the internal market by all member states, and enabled the Commission to embark on a major effort to develop an internal energy market as well as elements of a common energy policy. Energy markets were to be made transparent, infrastructure opened up to third-party suppliers, and investment and energy prices were to be reported and made available to the public. Given the monopoly status of many energy companies, the EC took on a very difficult task indeed.

2

Energy Policies in the EU Countries

Introduction: the structural parameters

Historically there has been very little energy policy cooperation at the European level. National policy has been dominated by the need to safeguard supplies by having diverse sources and ensuring the strategic use of domestic resources. Energy policy has been regarded as 'high politics' akin to security policy. Since energy is a main factor of production in all economies, its supply is of vital national importance.

However major changes are taking place in the energy sectors of the main EU countries, due partly to pressure at the EU level and partly to a general trend towards market liberalisation in former public sectors. In this chapter we look at the energy sectors of various EU states in order to provide a basis for the subsequent analysis of policy-making at the EU level. The parameters of energy policy in these states are explored, as well as the organisation of the energy sectors, the role of interest groups and government energy policy.

There has always been a marked difference between the political interests of energy-importing and energy-producing countries. We start with a brief analysis of the role that energy producers play in Europe and continue with an analysis of the energy policies of the main EU countries, all of which import at least some of their energy requirements (Table 2.1). Importing countries have the problem of securing reliable supplies, and share a common interest in a policy that will safeguard those supplies. Producing countries typically have different interests: they want the freedom to export as they deem profitable, and therefore typically seek to avoid common policies at

25

the EU level. Producers sometimes form an alliance, as in OPEC, an international cartel formed to control oil prices, but within Europe there is no formal cooperation of this type. Importers cooperate within the IEA, which provides an emergency oil-sharing mechanism.

Norway and Britain are the main producers of oil in Europe; Norway and the Netherlands are major suppliers of gas to the Continent. Oil is sold on the world market and thus there are no direct ties between producer and importer. For gas, however, there is the physical link of pipelines between gas field and end user. Three non-member countries are major gas exporters to the EU: Norway, Russia and Algeria.

Ensuring supply is not only a question of diversification of having more than one supplier, it also requires consideration of the political stability of the suppliers (Estrada, 1988; Stern, 1990). Gas is traded in contracts that last up to thirty years, and therefore there must be a relationship of trust between exporter and importer (Davis, 1984). With oil there is a need to be concerned about dependence on any one region, usually the Middle East. Security of supply has always

TABLE 2.1

Oil imports and production in the EU (mtoe)

	Net oil imports			
	1979	1993	2000 (projected)	Oil production (estimated)
Austria	11.4	10.1	10.8	0.8
Belgium	29.5	25.3	23	–
Britain	19.2	−17.9	5.7	97.0
Denmark	15.8	1.2	−0.8	9.9
Finland	14.9	9.0	11.4	–
France	123.7	87.1	94.6	1.0
Germany	166.6	133.9	138.4	1.0
Greece	13.3	16.6	19.3	–
Ireland	6.4	5.1	5.8	–
Italy	102.8	86.4	83.0	6.0
Luxembourg	1.4	2.0	1.9	–
Netherlands	41.5	32.9	34.5	2.0
Portugal	9.2	13.0	14.7	–
Spain	49.7	52.6	58.3	1.0
Sweden	29.4	16.3	17.5	–

Source: Adapted from *Energy Policies of IEA Countries* (Paris: IEA/OECD, 1994).

been a primary concern of national energy policies, and it is now becoming a prominent one on the EU agenda.

Of the other fuel types, both nuclear energy and coal are used widely in Europe (Table 2.2). Several European countries have a fuel structure that includes nuclear energy: foremost here is France, the leading producer of nuclear-generated electricity, but Germany, Belgium and Britain are partially dependent on domestically produced nuclear energy. Coal is the traditional European fuel, and it remains important even if production is dwindling. Germany still has a very important coal sector, and Spain and Britain are also coal producers. As we have seen, coal policy formed the basis of the first European treaty, the ECSC, and nuclear energy formed the basis of the second, Euratom.

National energy policies have clearly dominated European energy policy since the Second World War, and in major ways limit what is possible in the EU context in this field. An understanding of the role of national governments in this area is therefore essential to any analysis of EU energy policy. As stated, there are basic structural

TABLE 2.2

Energy use by sector, 1992

	Total energy demand (mtoe)	Solid fuel (%)	Oil (%)	Gas (%)	Nuclear (%)	Other (%)
Austria	25.9	23.8	43.7	20.8	–	11.8
Belgium	51.9	19.1	41.6	17.4	21.8	0.1
Britain	216.2	27.8	38.6	23.2	9.5	0.9
Denmark	19.4	41.6	45.4	11.0	–	2.1
Finland	28.0	32.4	33.6	8.8	17.9	7.2
France	231.2	9.9	39.3	12.1	38.1	0.5
Germany	340.3	31.3	39.5	16.7	12.2	0.3
Greece	22.9	38.1	60.3	0.6	–	1.1
Ireland	10.2	32.9	47.9	18.6	–	0.7
Italy	159.1	8.5	59.7	25.8	–	6.1
Luxembourg	3.8	28.1	51.6	12.2	–	9.1
Netherlands	68.8	11.3	37.6	48.5	1.4	1.1
Portugal	17.8	22.5	74.6	–	–	2.9
Spain	94.2	22.5	54.1	6.2	15.4	1.8
Sweden	46.7	18.3	31.6	1.3	35.4	13.3

Source: Adapted from *Energy Policies in the IEA Countries* (Paris: IEA/OECD, 1993).

differences between EU countries with regard to energy – an importer necessarily has different interests from a producer – and these structural parameters place a large constraint on policy-makers. Energy is one of the areas where natural resources go a long way towards determining a state's interests and possibilities, but beyond this there is room for various political courses of action (Samuels, 1987) as will become evident in this study.

In this analysis we are not only interested in the structural parameters of a given country's energy sector: its indigenous resources, supply dependence and import needs. We are also interested in the political structure of the energy sector (the role of the state and interest groups, the relationship between the government and energy companies, and so on) and the domestic energy policy agenda. Is, for instance, deregulation on that agenda, and can the government successfully oppose interest groups and energy companies when making national energy policy? The reason why this information is of importance to an analysis of EU energy policy is that governments will probably try to use the EU arena in the making domestic energy policy, to bring about deregulation for instance. As Putnam (1988) has pointed out, governments may invoke rules from international agreements, institutions and conventions to justify domestic policy measures, arguing that the government is bound to implement a certain policy despite local opposition (Putnam, 1988). As we shall see, EU governments have sometimes been able to capitalise on rulings in the European arena, but they have also been constrained by EU rules (Bulmer, 1983).

In the following we pay particular attention to four EU members – France, Germany, Britain and Italy – because they are the main actors in energy policy in the EU as well as in the EU in general. Although an in-depth study of all the member states is beyond the scope of this book, in order to provide a comprehensive picture other EU countries are covered in terms of their main energy parameters.

The producers: The Netherlands, Denmark and Britain

Energy parameters

The Netherlands is a large gas exporter to the rest of the EU. In 1959 the enormous Groningen gas field was discovered, and from this field large parts of the EU have been supplied with gas for more than twenty years. In fact the natural gas era in Europe can be said to have started because of this field. Until the 1960s was used only in towns and was produced locally. Natural gas can however be transported in high-pressure, long-distance pipelines, and its discovery stimulated the development of a regional gas market. Today gas amounts to some 20 per cent of total primary energy consumption in Europe, and until recently Dutch gas made up the largest share of this.

Dutch gas production peaked in 1970 at over 100 bcm (billion cubic metres), falling to about 70 bcm by 1990. Of the latter amount, 40–50 bcm is used domestically and the rest is exported to other EU countries. The export volume is expected to settle at 40 bcm in the first decades of the next century. It is anticipated that Norway will become the largest European exporter of gas to continental Europe, closely followed by the Netherlands. Russia will remain the largest of all suppliers, with exports of about 90 bcm per year to the EU and Central Europe, although Algerian exports through a pipeline to Italy are expected to be substantial.

Denmark too is a net exporter of natural gas, mainly to southern Sweden and to a lesser extent Germany. The exported amount is small: 1.47 bcm in 1992, or 23 per cent of production. Production in 1993 rose slightly. Denmark is 98 per cent self-sufficient in oil.

Another major European energy-producing and exporting country is *Britain*. In 1992 Britain had a net oil export of 9.2 mtoe (million tons of oil equivalent) out of a total production of 94 mtoe. Natural gas was exported in small quantities to the Netherlands, but the bulk was used domestically. Britain is largely self-sufficient in energy.

Energy sector organisation: Britain

Between 1980 and 1990, Britain made dramatic changes to its energy sector in line with its overall economic policy (Nelson, 1993). The state-owned fuel industries were privatised, starting with oil and gas and continuing with electricity and coal. As indicated, this privatisation programme was not specific to the energy sector, but was part of the general privatisation drive of the Thatcher government (Swann, 1989). Previously the presence of the state in the energy sector had been highly pervasive – all the major energy providers were in public hands, including gas and oil (Robinson,

1982) – but now all but the nuclear section of the electricity industry have been privatised.

The government still regulates the market to a certain extent through licensing, environmental and safety controls as well as through fiscal measures. However one of the main aims of the government's programme – the promotion of competition – has not automatically resulted from deregulation. Rather the government has had to intervene to create the conditions for competition, especially in the gas and electricity sectors.

The British Gas Corporation a former monopolist, was privatised in 1986. The new company, British Gas, is still obliged to supply the tariff market (smaller consumers) but there is competition in the non-tariff market. There are now some 30 companies supplying customers in this market, and they are entitled to use the grid owned by British Gas.

In order to ensure competition the government has had to make rules to force British Gas to reduce its share of the market. Deregulation and privatisation were vigorously opposed by the British Gas Corporation and most of the rest of the energy industry as they wished to retain their public status but the government was in a sufficiently strong position to withstand this opposition and pressed ahead regardless.

Once privatised British Gas tried to retain ownership of the gas grid. There ensued a Monopolies and Merger Commission report on the conflict between the government-appointed regulatory body, Ofgas (Office of Gas Competition), and British Gas. Its conclusion was that British Gas should not own a transmission system used by its competitors. In addition the Secretary of State for Trade and Industry announced that the monopoly on gas supply to the tariff market should be abolished by 1996–97, with 50 per cent of the market being opened to competition each year. (This also happened in the electricity market.) There is thus no public service function at work in the gas sector and the government is present only through the regulator, Ofgas.

Privatisation of the publicly owned coal industry started in 1994 with the massive restructuring of the national coal company, British Coal, in preparation for market liberalisation.

In the electricity sector the privatisation of two electricity companies took place in 1991 – National Power and PowerGen. The government has instituted a regulatory body for electricity, OFFER, which oversees competition in this sector. Nuclear energy has not been privatised because of the problems with decommissioning and waste.

Government policy: Britain

The official goals of British energy policy are to encourage competition and shed government responsibility. As stated above, for quite sometime privatisation has been a general aim for government policy and is not specific to the energy sector (Hall, 1986), thus energy policy is part of general economic policy. In an annual review of member states policies the IEA remarked that 'The UK has an energy policy in the sense that it is part of market liberalisation' (IEA, 1994a, p. 485). The government intervenes only to make the market function better, for instance in order to create the conditions for competition in the gas and electricity sectors. It has shown no particular interest in retaining control of the sector by indirect means (Stern, 1987), although through Ofgas it has instituted measures to ensure that competition develops in gas provision and to control the price of transmission.

Interest groups in the energy sector were unenthusiastic about privatisation and all the public companies resisted such as move, however, the government paid no heed.

In the development of environmental policy with implications for the energy sector, general reliance on market forces is a central feature: 'one consequence has been an interest in market mechanisms for achieving environmental goals' (Grubb, 1991, p. 210). Thus energy saving and energy efficiency schemes are key elements of the government's environmental strategy, which includes the stabilisation of CO_2 emissions at the 1990 level by the year 2005. Here the British government has insisted on full national control and does not accept an EU role beyond that of coordination.

In summary the British government pursued a strategy of general privatisation despite opposition from the energy sector. There is little evidence of a government aimed specifically at the energy sector and domestic energy interests. It is promoting competition in this sector, as in other parts of the economy, having divested the economy of many public responsibilities. This development represents a massive shift away from British state capitalism (Shonfield, 1967; Heritier, 1994; Lucas, 1985).

The importers: Germany, France and Italy

Energy parameters: Germany

Germany is a large importer, a substantial producer and an transporter of energy in the EU. Its energy consumption was just below 250 mtoe in 1993, having fallen slightly because of the closure of many old industries in the new *Länder*. In 1994 Germany imported 78 per cent of its gas and 99 per cent of its oil requirements. Supply security and source diversification therefore loom large in national energy policy. As much of the gas comes from Russia, Germany is bound to diversify with imports from other sources.

Domestically coal produced is in decline in both the old and the new *Länder* (Prognos, 1989). To offset this decline as well as importing oil and gas, the domestic production of nuclear energy is being slowly increased. It is forecast that the energy mix will undergo major changes before 2010: lignite production will drop by 11 per cent and gas imports will rise by 6 per cent (IEA, 1993). Much of the anticipated gas increase will be met by Norway.

Energy sector organisation: Germany

There is no uniform energy sector in Germany in terms of organisation and government involvement (Héritier, 1994; Lucas, 1985). The role of the state in the coal and nuclear sectors is a major one, whereas the oil sector is governed by free-market rules. In the gas sector the market is divided between different actors (Estrada, 1988; Davis, 1984). Energy policy is determined not only by government but also by the *Länder*, since Germany is a federal political system (von Beyme, 1983). There is thus a decentralised structure of decision-making with specific competences at various levels (Bulmer and Paterson, 1996; Heritier, 1994) , as well as sharp differences in organisation between the energy forms. Energy policy is limited by legal rulings on prices, markets, supply obligations and so on for gas and electricity that date back several decades (*Energierecht*, 1964).

In the gas sector there is a 'shared market' system (*geordneter Markt*), which divides the market into sections dominated by different companies. However this system, which has evolved over a long time (Lucas, 1985), is gradually being changed. The two parts of Germany now share a single grid system, which is also connected to Central

Europe – Germany is the key transporter of Russian gas through major pipelines to other parts of Europe. The gas pipelines are privately owned, including the ones that transport gas from third countries through Germany.

In the new *Länder* massive privatisation of all energy forms has taken place, for example *Verbundnetz Gas* of former East Germany was bought by Ruhrgas and other international gas companies. Since reunification a number of new gas companies have been set up.

In the oil sector, private companies dominate and there is no government intervention or policy.

The coal sector is organised into private companies but the government remains the guarantor of coal subsidies. Domestically produced coal is more than three times the price of imported coal. German coal policy rests on two agreements between the government and the mining companies (notably the giant Ruhrkohle) – the so-called *Jahrhundertvertrag* – and with the steel industry – the *Hüttenvertrag*. Both these agreements deal with how the government will guarantee that coal mining will reach a certain level each year. Coal production was reduced by about 40 million tons a year in the latter half of the 1980s, yet the level of subsidies remains in the order of DM10–11 billion.

During the 1987 annual talks between the *Länder*, the mining companies and the government it was decided to reduce production by 15 million tons per year and increase the so-called *Kohlenpfennig* (a tax paid by consumers of electricity to sustain the coal industry) from 7.25 per cent to 8.5 per cent. However this decision was taken up by the German constitutional court, the *Bundesverfassungsgericht*, which ruled in late 1994 that it was illegal. The government thus needs to find other ways of funding its coal subsidies.

The nuclear sector in Germany is important but politically very controversial (Hatch, 1991). There are 21 nuclear plants, all in the old *Länder*, the ones in the new *Länder* having been shut down for safety reasons. A major debate on the future of nuclear energy was launched in 1991, when an energy policy document, 'The Energy Concept', was published. So-called 'consensus' talks between the Ministries of Economics and Environment then started. These all-party talks collapsed in late 1993 because the Social-Democratic Party (SPD) stuck to its 'no nuclear' position and the Greens were actively in opposed to the entire nuclear industry. The political uncertainty surrounding the future of nuclear energy has led to a halt in investment.

Government policy: Germany

German energy policy is characterised by a curious mixture of market reliance and strong state intervention (Kuster, 1974). Trade in oil and gas is left largely to the market, whereas the state plays a significant role in coal and nuclear power. As stated above, energy policy is decided by both the Ministry of Economics and the *Lander* and legal ruling determine the rights and duties of each level. An official of the *Bundeskartellamt* summarised German energy policy thus: 'We don't have a national energy policy in Germany in terms of day-to-day public interference. We should think of our national energy policy in terms of a general consensus that has been reached by all parties, including a special role for coal and a diversification of supply' (interview, Brussels, 1992).

The major policy goals are laid out in the 1991 'Energy Concept' document: security of supply, cost-effectiveness, diversification, environmental compatibility and market-based approaches to solving energy problems. However an important review by the IEA made the criticism that: 'German energy policy is still underpinned by major rigidities: the coal policy, the demarcation and concession system in the electricity and gas sectors and the lack of consensus concerning nuclear power . . . major energy policy decisions are likely to be postponed' (IEA, 1994a, p. 263). The IEA's criticism is particularly strong with regard to coal policy: 'An overall rethinking of the traditional German approach [to coal policy] would seem to be urgently needed. . . . The slow pace of restructuring in the hard coal industry is in striking contrast with the restructuring of the lignite industry in the new Länder' and 'The German government should reduce direct and indirect subsidies to hard coal production' (ibid., p. 266). Likewise, in the gas sector 'The government should examine ways to strengthen the competitive elements in the gas market and pursue consideration of proposed amendments to energy-related legislation' (ibid., p. 267). The IEA also points to the lack of clear policy direction with regard to nuclear energy.

In the 1980s the environment became a prime domestic issue and a major theme in energy policy. In the 1990s environmental questions have dominated the energy debate. For example a report commissioned by the Ministry of Economics to analyse future energy trends in Germany noted that, 'new problem areas have come to the fore in comparison with previous years. This is especially true of the increasing environmental repercussions arising from energy production and use' (German Enquete Commission, 1990). Germany has passed some of Europe's most stringent environmental laws, and has developed technology in this field to an advanced level. Standards for car emissions are now higher in Germany than those required by the EU.

Gas accounts for only 5 per cent of electricity generation in Germany, whereas the controversial energy source coal represents 55 per cent. Coal increased its share in the power market from 39 per cent in 1981 to 54 per cent in 1987. The subsidisation of coal is a major area of conflict in domestic German energy policy as well as between the German government and the European Commission. Support for the coal industry forms part of German social and employment policy rather than energy policy since imported coal is much cheaper than that mined domestically.

The federal structure of the German polity makes the existence of a strongly centralised state elite in any sector almost impossible. The competition and merger rules, for instance are largely managed by the *Bundeskartellamt* and the government has little to do directly with this. Officially the government supports the idea of an EU internal energy market, but – according to Padgett (1992) only because it supports the internal market in general. As part of the general trend towards deregulation, the Economics Ministry set up a working group in 1988 to review the *geordneter Markt* practice in the energy sector (see above). The intention was to 'push back the influence of the state', and if possible the working group was to suggest ways of bringing about deregulation. However the Ministry warned that it had no intention of 'breaking away from the tried and tested model of [German] competition law (cited in ibid., p. 66). Within the Ministry the energy policy division maintained that the nature of the energy sector justified a *geordneter Markt* and opposed any move towards an EU internal energy market. Another section of the Ministry, that dealing with general economic policy, disagreed. The influence of interest groups on the energy policy division was, in Padgett's view, the reason for this difference of opinion.

In summary, the German government is not an autonomous energy policy actor because of the decentralised structure of the political system, the lack of a common energy policy and the lack of uniformity in the organisation of the sector.

Energy parameters: France

France is a net importer of energy (Table 2.3). It imports almost all of its oil, as well as 95 per cent of gas and 76 per cent of its coal requirements. Fear of excessive dependence on any one import source has therefore always ranked highly in France's energy concerns. The development of nuclear energy has been the logical response to this situation. Nuclear energy today makes up 36 per cent of primary energy consumption, while oil stands at 39 per cent. Gas and coal make up 12 per cent and 8 per cent respectively.

There are some national gas fields, notably the large Lacq field, but most oil and gas is imported. Domestic oil production continues to decline, although France has important resources. Gas production is also declining, and imports are on the rise. Russia and Algeria are the main sources of gas, followed by Norway. Coal production too has fallen due to the closure of unprofitable mines, although coal is still important in electricity generation (Table 2.4). The state-owned coal company, Charbonnages de France, has reported large losses and is subsidised by EU grants to alleviate the cost of retraining former miners. The government and Charbonnages de France have agreed that all unprofitable mines should be closed by 2005.

The nuclear sector is the main one in France in terms of domestic production. There are new plants under construction, but no additional ones are planned.

Energy sector organisation: France

France has a very strong tradition of state ownership of energy companies (Feigenbaum, 1985; Lucas, 1977, 1985), all of which were nationalised in 1946. Only recently have liberalisation and privatisation become key policy objectives. How to restructure the energy sector has been a major preoccupation in French energy policy in recent years, and in 1993 the government set up a group to assess the problem. The group also looked at whether to retain the law from 1946 that gave monopoly rights to Électricité de France and Gaz de France. However, 'This move was largely in response to pressure from the EC to remove *de jure* monopoly rights for the import and export of electricity' (IEA, 1993).

The group's report, called the Mandil Report, was published in 1994. It recommended the removal of monopoly rights and the creation of a separate regulatory body for the electricity and gas

TABLE 2.3

Total net imports (mtoe) 1992

	Total	Coal	Oil	Gas	Electr.	Domestic prod.
Austria	17.9	3.1	10.3	4.3	0.0	8.7
Belgium	40.2	9.4	21.6	9.1	0.0	12.2
Britain	5.5	9.6	−12.7	7.4	1.1	212.5
Denmark	7.0	7.3	0.6	−1.3	0.3	12.7
Finland	15.3	3.3	8.8	2.5	0.7	11.7
France	122.5	14.2	86.3	26.6	−4.6	116.6
Germany	186.9	9.5	133.6	44.4	−0.5	161.0
Greece	15.3	1.4	13.9	–	–	8.5
Ireland	7.1	2.2	4.8	–	–	3.2
Italy	133.6	12.1	90.1	28.3	3.0	27.5
Luxembourg	3.8	1.0	1.9	0.4	0.3	–
Netherlands	2.6	7.4	23.1	−2.6	0.7	66.7
Portugal	16.1	2.8	13.2	–	0.1	1.5
Spain	63.8	9.3	49.6	4.8	0.1	30.9
Sweden	16.9	2.2	14.3	0.6	−0.2	29.1

Source: Adapted from *Review of Energy Policies* (Paris: IEA/OECD, 1994).

TABLE 2.4

Electricity Generation – percentage share of fuels, 1992

	Solid fuel	Oil	Gas	Nuclear	Hydro/ other
Austria	11.3	5.4	13.5	–	69.3
Belgium	27.2	2.2	9.3	60.8	0.5
Britain	62.7	8.5	2.7	24.1	2.0
Denmark	90.8	3.6	2.5	–	3.0
Finland	29.1	2.0	8.9	33.6	26.4
France	8.5	2.1	0.7	73.9	14.9
Germany	58.3	2.5	6.2	29.8	3.3
Greece	71.5	22.4	0.2	–	5.9
Ireland	56.0	15.7	23.1	–	5.2
Italy	11.6	52.1	15.8	–	20.5
Luxembourg	76.4	8.5	4.5	–	10.6
Netherlands	34.3	4.2	56.2	4.9	0.3
Portugal	37.6	46.8	–	–	15.7
Spain	42.0	9.2	1.1	35.6	12.1
Sweden	3.2	1.6	0.5	43.6	51.1

Source: Adapted from *Review of Energy Policies* (Paris: IEA/OECD, 1994).

industries. According to the report, Électricité de France should lose its monopoly on generation, and both companies should only partially retain their import and export monopoly rights. There should be a regulator to oversee deregulated industries, but both companies should retain their public service functions. General third-party access is precluded because the companies should retain control over transmission and distribution, with the possible exception of some large industrial actors. The Mandil Report resulted in a major debate on energy-sector organisation in France, and there were large protests in the streets against privatisation as it would probably entail the loss of jobs. The argument is that the public service function is endangered.

The gas sector's import monopoly should be alleviated, according to the Mandil Report, but the negotiations over gas imports should be coordinated with Gaz de France. Regional transportation companies need no longer be state-owned, and municipalities hooking up to the grid should have a choice of supplier. This is a major change from the 1946 law, which gave Gaz de France monopoly rights in this respect.

While Gaz de France is wholly state-owned, there are regional gas companies that are owned by Gaz de France and other companies, such as the Société nationale de gaz du Sud-Ouest, which is owned jointly by Elf (70 per cent) and Gaz de France (30 per cent), both of whom also have a 50 per cent share in Compagnie française de methane.

The gas industry is regulated by the Ministry of Industry, which grants transportation concessions to companies with at least 30 per cent state ownership. Tariffs to all but large industrial consumers are controlled by the government.

As for electricity, the Mandil Report's recommendations concern two major aspects: Électricité de France's monopoly rights over generation, and its monopoly rights over imports and exports. Électricité de France would be obliged to buy from all producers and the tariffs would be set by the public authorities. Although monopoly import–export rights would be removed, the government would retain authority over large imports and all exports in order to ensure that the national requirements are met. Hence there would be no free import–export right, as all importers would have to go through the public authorities. This is called the 'single buyer' (SB) model, which is central to EU decision-making and will therefore be discussed in later chapters.

The oil companies have been partly privatised as part of the government's economic strategy. In early 1994 the government sold most of its shares in the gas and oil company Elf Aquitaine, raising over 30 billion francs, but the state retains a 'golden share'. Two years earlier it had reduced its participation in Total, the other major oil company, from 35 to 5 per cent.

Government policy: France

The main debate in France has been, and remains, the privatisation of the energy sector. However security of supply is also a major issue, and the commitment to nuclear energy continues. There is no agreement on how far privatisation should go – the state's share of the French energy companies is still large and there has been very strong opposition to privatisation by the companies themselves and the trade unions, although this has been very modest compared with the situation in Britain. As will be seen later, the French government has been adamant about protecting its own version of partial privatisation (the SB model), and has battled with the EU Commission for several years on this issue.

Environmental policy is being tied to energy policy but this process is in its very beginnings. According to the IEA, 'Clearly defined objectives and a plan for meeting environmental and efficiency goals are still needed' (IEA, 1994, p. 237).

Energy parameters: Italy

Italy is energy–poor and imports most of its coal, oil and gas. Oil imports make up about 95 per cent of total oil supplies and imported gas accounted for 66 per cent of gas use in 1992. The major gas supplier is Algeria, with 42.8 per cent in 1992. Italy is also the major transit country for Algerian gas to other parts of Europe. Over 99 per cent of coal supplies are imported. There is no nuclear sector in Italy as a result of a moratorium imposed after a referendum in 1987.

Energ sector organisation: Italy

Traditionally the energy sector in Italy has been state-owned. ENI, the major holding company, has several subsidiaries that deal with various aspects of the energy sector. As a consequence of the EU's internal market legislation as well as the general trend towards privatisation, ENI is being gradually privatised. A law authorising the privatisation of major public companies was passed in 1992 marking the end of an era of very pervasive state ownership in Italian economic life (Lucas, 1985).

ENEL, the public electricity company, will eventually be fully privatised, but some restrictions may be imposed for the first few years. ENEL will retain its monopoly rights over the transmission of electricity and to a great extent its distribution, and it will remain a public company with a public service function. The government plans to establish a regulatory body to supervise prices and deregulation. There is no plan to break up the company in separate entities.

Government policy: Italy

Italian energy policy is set out the *plan energetico nazionale* (national energy plan). In 1991 there was a new plan that which signalled a major shift from central planning to a liberal market approach, in line with EU developments and domestic thinking on deregulation. For a country where the energy sector had been wholly state-owned for such a long time, this was a remarkable development.

Since Italy is so dependent on imported fuel there is a strong emphasis on energy efficiency. This is also good in relation to environmental protection, which is another of Italy's main goals, along with development of the few indigenous resources that do exist, diversification of suppliers and increased competitiveness of the supply systems. The IEA comments that 'The government has made headway in restructuring ENI and ENEL in preparation for priva-tisation and in establishing a new regulatory framework, including a concession agreement for ENEL and the planned creation of a separate government body to streamline regulation of the electricity supply industry' (IEA, 1994, p. 325). However the Italian political system remains fragile (Farneti, 1985) and the phenomenon known as *sotto-governo* is pervasive – this refers to the large degree of autonomy that sub-government sectors and public companies have traditionally had in Italy.

The small importers: Austria, Belgium, Finland, Sweden and Luxembourg

Austria, Finland and Sweden joined the EU in 1995 and of course had no impact on EU energy policy prior to accession. They are all energy importers and will probably side with that group on energy matters at the EU level. The smaller importers are most likely to favour a fairly strong hand on the part of the Commission in EU policy. It should be noted that the two new Nordic countries place strong emphasis on the environmental aspect of energy policy. Furthermore, they are both consumers and producers of nuclear energy and their energy structure differs markedly from that of their neighbours – Norway and Denmark, which are energy-rich and exporters of petroleum.

Austria is in the fortunate position of being able to fulfil a large proportion of its domestic energy needs hydro-electrically (65–70 per cent of electricity use). Biomass has a large share of total energy consumption (11 per cent). Almost all oil, gas and coal is imported. Austria is an 'umbilical cord' for the importation of gas from Russia, and a pipeline is currently being constructed between Baumgarten in Austria and Gyor in Hungary in order to link Hungary to the Western grid. Austria is also a key transit country for westbound Russian gas, and is thus in a position to increase its gas supply without constructing additional infrastructure.

Import of fuel is essential to *Belgium* – there are no indigenous fossil fuels and the last coal mine was closed in 1992. Less than 24 per cent of the total energy demand is met by domestic supplies, and here nuclear-generated electricity makes up the lion's share. There are no plans to increase the share of nuclear energy, however, as gas imports are set to increase. Belgium strongly favours EU-level and international policies in energy, and has called for the development of a common EU energy policy.

Finland relies heavily on gas imported from Russia and has no domestic deposits of fossil fuels. Nuclear energy makes up 18 per cent of primary energy consumption – the rest of the electricity supply is water-generated. Coal use fell by 20 per cent between 1990 and 1992, and this largely accounted for a 5 per cent decrease in CO_2 emissions. In 1993 Finland signed a contract for additional supplies of gas from Russia. The 'Finnish Energy Strategy' from 1992 sets out three goals: security of supply, market efficiency and limitation of emissions. Carbon taxes and 'no regrets' policies have been developed in detail in Finland.

Sweden satisfies an important share of its energy requirement with nuclear electricity, which together with hydro-electricity makes for reductions in emissions as well as accounting for a high proportion of the domestic energy supply. Whether or not to retain the nuclear sector was the subject of a 1980 referendum. Although nuclear power was decided against no action was taken. Instead an agreement between various corporate and political actors in the energy sector was reached in 1991, to postpone the phasing out of nuclear energy until 'an appropriate time'. This has been interpreted to mean an informal reversal of the referendum. CO_2 production must thus be met by other means. This appears very unlikely to happen, as nuclear power makes up 44 per cent of the electricity supply Sweden imports small amounts of natural gas from Denmark and all of its oil from other external sources.

Dependent on energy imports from Belgium as well as vulnerable to transfrontier pollution, *Luxembourg* strongly supports a common EU energy and environmental policy. The national energy plan emphasises energy saving and improved efficiency. Reduced energy consumption will meet the twin goals of reducing both energy imports and atmospheric emissions.

The 'cohesion' countries: Ireland, Greece, Spain and Portugal

It is anticipated that energy consumption will grow in the years ahead. Their aim to promote economic growth implies increased energy use, and the other EU countries are agreed that a common CO_2 tax will not apply to these countries until they have reached a level of economic development that is comparable to that of the richer countries. However there is no agreement on how to determine this level, and no serious discussion of this extremely difficult topic has yet been undertaken. If the EU is going to develop a common environmental policy the issue of 'burden sharing' among the member states will have to be addressed in detail.

Another common feature of the energy sector in these countries is the lack of modern infrastructure. Since the energy sector is relatively underdeveloped in large parts of these countries, much can be done in terms of modernisation and efficient technology to develop the sector, including the extension of gas and electricity grids. There are important EU programmes and funds to help in this respect. The 'cohesion' countries are energy-poor and thus depend heavily on imports.

In *Ireland* imported fuel amounted to more than 70 per cent of the total energy requirement in 1994, and this will increase after 2005 when the domestic sources of gas are depleted. The other domestic energy sources are electricity and peat. Ireland wants additional gas infrastructure, including a pipeline from Britain.

The expected growth in energy use in *Greece* is formidable: while it doubled from 1973 to 1992, it will increase by another 70 per cent by 2005. Nearly 80 per cent of energy is imported, and this share will also increase to 82 per cent by 2005. The only domestic fossil is lignite, which is scheduled to increase its share in primary energy consumption.

More than 90 per cent of energy is imported in *Portugal*, and in dry years there is a shortfall in hydro-electricity, which means that fuel oil must compensate. Energy use is expected to increase substantially, especially in the transport sector. There is also a pressing need for improved infrastructure.

Spain imports all its oil, 83 per cent of its gas and more than 45 per cent of its coal. Domestic nuclear generation will decrease as the result of a moratorium on the construction of further facilities. Importing gas from Algeria will become a possibility with the completion of a pipeline to Gibraltar.

Conclusions

EU countries vary considerably in energy structure and this affects their energy policy. There are national policy traditions on state versus market that largely determine how the energy sectors have been structured, and the availability of domestic fuel supplies plays a major role in this. The interests of importing countries differ from those of exporting countries, but the majority of EU members are importers.

Differences in the level of economic development represent a major cleavage in terms of energy policy: while the rich north concerns itself with the effects of market deregulation, the poorer south seeks economic growth through the development of an energy sector and infrastructure with the help of EU aid.

Of the four states under special consideration here, Italy has done the least to deregulate its domestic energy sector. The government is constrained by a large public energy sector that is not responsive to major change. In contrast the British government was able to carry out its deregulation and privatisation programme despite opposition from the energy sector. In Germany there has been a general pattern of decentralised decision-making in the energy sector, with wide variations in the roles of the government and the *Länder* in various areas of the sector. Coal continues to play a major role in German politics, whereas nuclear energy has become politically unacceptable. In the oil and gas sectors market actors prevail, and the gas market is divided between the major companies in a system called *geordneter Markt.*

In France the government still has a strong hand in the energy sector, despite some attempts at deregulation, and has a major interest in retaining a strong nuclear energy capability.

Apart from the Netherlands and Denmark, all the other EU countries are net importers of energy. Only Britain is really committed to a free market philosophy in the energy sector.

In sum there are no 'natural' groups of member states with common energy interests beyond the classification of importer–exporter, although there is a clear north–south divide in terms of energy infrastructure and modern facilities.

3

The Internal Energy
Market

Introduction: the Commission as regulator

In this chapter we present in detail the proposals for an internal
energy market, with special emphasis on deregulation within the
larger European context. The current degree of deregulation varies
widely between countries, and although many public sector companies are resisting such a move, the idea of an IEM would hardly have
been feasible without major support for general deregulation on the
part of the EU member governments.

The trend towards deregulation and the privatisation of former
public marked the end of traditional state capitalism, but it has not
always led to reduced state power in the management of the economy
(Majone, 1994). Rather, argues Majone, the state has attained a new
role – that of regulator. A regulator typically does not need a large
budget, but it does need considerable technical insight into the areas
it oversees as well as strong legal intervention instruments. According
to Majone (ibid.), the EU Commission is perfectly equipped to be an
efficient regulator: not only does it dispose of strong legal tools in
competition legislation, it also has the exclusive right of policy
initiative and thus of designing a policy process. It can invite
participants and is the drafter of texts; in short it is a 'policy
entrepreneur'. The political power inherent in this is potentially very
great, an insight that has been so far neglected by theorists of
European integration, according to Majone. The power of the
Commission is thus not the traditional power of states.

In the following we look at how work on the internal energy
market has progressed, bearing in mind that deregulation does not

necessarily imply a 'rolling back of the state', or of the Commission's role. In Chapter 6 the relative roles of the Commission and other actors are evaluated; here we focus on how the Commission has defined the IEM and how effective it has been in creating a regulatory role for itself.

The Commission has always tried to bring about a consensus on controversial issues, and sometimes this has led to substantial compromises after several years of negotiation. In the event of complete deadlock the Commission has tended to invoke competition legislation, which can be applied directly by the Competition Directorate. Both Sir Leon Brittan and Karel van Miert, competition commissioners during the formative years of the internal market, were committed to the intensive application of competition legislation to the energy sector, and it has remained a favourite tool of energy commissioners whenever there has been a serious deadlock in the Council of Ministers over an energy issue. Competition policy is thus a major source of political power for the Commission.

Deregulation and reregulation

Throughout the deliberations over the internal market in general there has been a conflict between the *de*regulation of markets – the push for more market and less politics – and the call for reregulation, where the reordering of markets can result in a greater political presence. This is perhaps a question of national political styles – the British want a *laissez-faire* market, the Germans a *geordneter Markt* and the French more *dirigisme*. The existence of national policy styles and their importance for EU policy-making is well documented (Héritier *et al.*, 1994). There are undoubtedly major differences of opinion as to what role the EU institutions should play in the future internal market. For example should the Commission be an active watchdog, or rather a casual observer once the work of reordering is done?

The degree to which a market presupposes political monitoring – concentrated in Brussels – is thus a major bone of contention between the member states. The tension between those who want fewer Brussels-based powers of intervention and those who want more power to ensure the market rules are followed is evident, for instance, in the discussion over how the EU can ensure that third parties are allowed to exercise their right to use gas pipelines owned by others. Some are opting for a controlling bureaucracy in Brussels, others balk at this idea, fearing that it will lead to even more political intervention and bureaucratic slowdown.

However the change of rules that the IEM represents is a reregulation in the sense that these changes will be imposed on often reluctant market actors by politicians. If the result of rule change is a freer market, it makes sense to speak of deregulation. Thus the contents of the proposals may be called deregulatory, yet the political process of rule change itself is a reregulation (Majone, 1990). Dehousse argues that deregulation in the EU often implies an enhanced political role for the Commission (Dehousse, 1992).

Since 1988 the Commission has made several proposals for the creation of an IEM that goes beyond a simple IEM in scope and implies a policy-making role for the Commission. The following may be classified as IEM proposals:

- Harmonisation of indirect taxation.
- Price and investment transparency.
- Competition for public procurement.
- Third-party access to oil and gas.
- Integration of electricity and gas grids.
- Application of competition legislation to the upstream part of oil and gas exploration and production.
- Restructuring of state aid for coal.

However the next set of proposals demand an institutional energy policy

- Plans for an EU policy of supply security by the year 2005.
- A European Energy Charter.
- The official merging of energy and environmental policy from 1990.
- Amendment proposals for the inclusion of energy in the treaty text.

Some of the measures that pertain to the internal market in general have a direct bearing on energy policy, for instance state policy with respect to coal subsidies and R&D policies. Also of importance is a directive on public procurement that includes the energy sector (COM88/377).

The first IEM proposals from the Energy Directorate were introduced as a package in late 1989: price transparency in the electricity and gas sectors was the subject of a communication in March 1989

(COM 89/123); proposals for and transmission of gas (COM89/334) and electricity (COM89/336) were set forth at the same time, along with plans for the monitoring of large investments in the energy sector. The fuel transmission directives were adopted in 1989 and 1990 respectively, but the directive for the piping of natural gas was so extensively modified that the Commission drafted a new directive in 1991, which promoted the same idea of open access to pipelines, but this time in a more radical fashion. One called for general third party access, that is, all energy actors should have access to the pipelines. In other words, what the Commission failed to achieve in the 1989 directives in terms of market liberalisation it tried to bring about in a new effort two years later.

A major conflict between the EU governments and the Commission erupted in 1990, over the issue of third party access to the for gas and electricity networks. Third party access, also called common carriage, means that all suppliers should have access to gas pipelines and electricity grids, subject to the payment of a tariff set by some independent authority. This is the same principle as that which applies to other forms of transportation, and is an essential element of the internal market. However in the energy sector, the gas and electricity networks are often owned by energy companies that see the imposition of third party access as unjustified intervention in their commercial activity and are resisting it vigorously. In the gas sector it is very much feared that third party access would undermine long-term stability of supply since customers would be reluctant to enter into long-term contracts if the production and transportation of gas were to be decoupled.

Common to all the proposals for third-party access is that the process should take place in two stages: first, grid owners would be allowed access to other grids; later, third parties could be included. Requests for access would have to be passed on to the Commission, which would monitor the process. If no contract resulted after a year of negotiating, the Commission would be able to intervene. This could mean invoking Article 86 or 90, the Treaty of Rome, which allow the Commission to take action against, *inter alia*, state-owned monopolies that hinder competition.

To settle commercial and technological disputes the Commission would set up panels of experts, consisting of EU representatives and industry spokesmen. Typical issues could be determining the spare capacity of networks and establishing a just price for third party access.

Third party access to electricity grids was adopted by the Council of Energy Ministers in a modifed form in October 1990. The gas transmission directive was informally adopted at the same meeting, but the text needed further clarification. Germany and the Netherlands were the only two countries to vote against the proposals. (The process of policy adoption is analysed in Chapters 5 and 6.)

In the summer of 1991 the Commission started to formalise the work that had been carried out by working groups on the internal market for electricity and gas. At the end of the year a communication on further work towards the IEM was published, wherein the Commission outlined a progressive evolution towards open third party access to these markets – the adoption of the 1989 directives on gas and electricity distribution was deemed 'the *first* step towards establishing an internal gas and electricity market', and the Commission now desired to step up this work (interview, 1993).

This was an extremely controversial proposal, and before its launch four consultative groups, consisting of representatives of interest groups and national experts, had worked on its implications – the proposal was 'the result of lengthy consultation with national administration and the circles concerned' (*Europe*, January 1992). These groups had met monthly for more than a year and had produced four reports with their views on the proposals. The Commission had thus tried to ensure support for its proposal through the co-option of actors, wide-ranging discussions and expert analysis.

The Commission went on to outline the many obstacles that could obstruct the development of an IEM in these sectors. There must be progress towards increased competition, but this should be done in stages: since the actors in these markets would need time to adjust the changes should be introduced gradually – 'laying down a minimum level of liberalisation to be achieved at each stage', as one official put it. However the Commission would not impose a given regime on the market actors. Here the principle of subsidiarity was invoked, allotting quite a large degree of freedom to each member state: 'The Community must not impose rigid mechanisms, but rather should define a framework enabling member states to opt for the system best suited to their national resources, the state of their industry and their energy policies'. A third principle was that the Commission would avoid 'excessive regulation': any new regulatory measures should replace and not add to the existing body of rules. This was designed to appease those that fear the Commission will establish a major regulatory role for itself.

Completing the IEM will entail (1) putting into force the previously adopted transmission directives; (2) 'unbundling' the different operations in the sector, that is, separating the transmission and distribution functions in order to facilitate the application of rules of competition; and (3) the introduction of limited third party access, mainly to large industrial customers and distributors. Again the Commission stresses that member governments will retain major powers when it comes to the second stage, referring to the principle of subsidiarity.

The Commission based its new third party access proposals on Article 100a SEA, the internal market paragraph. This meant that the cooperation procedure would apply. It could have chosen Article 90, which gives the Commission the authority to intervene when competition is being hindered, but according to one commentator the Commission does not rule out the use of Article 90 at a later stage (*Europe*, 22 January 1992). However it was thought desirable to let the member states have the major say in matters as controversial as this proposal, although the formal power to intervene rests with the Commission alone.

The political process towards third party access to the electricity and gas markets continued from 1991 to 1995, when some progress on electricity was made. The Commission chose to work on electricity first as this was politically easier than dealing with gas. It hoped to establish a precedent with electricity, using precedents already established in other fields, such as telecommunications and transport. By the end of 1995 there was a Council agreement that the third party proposals would be modified to accommodate a French proposal called the single buyer model, which would allow a dominant position to be retained by Électricité de France, as recommended in the Mandil Report. However Britain wanted third party access in the form proposed by the Commission.

The Commission tried to accommodate both positions in a working paper issued in 1995, where it deemed that the single buyer model would be compatible with third party access if it were severely modifed. In autumn 1995 the Council agreed that both systems could coexist as reciprocal ones, although it was unable to work out the details of how this could be brought about. This outcome was seen as a victory for the French and also as a necessary concession on the part of the Commission. This agreement meant that progress was at last being made towards the liberalisation of electricity markets, but it had been an extremely long and arduous process in which the initial proposal by the Commission had been modified several times.

Strong interest groups and member governments have opposed many of the IEM proposals. However the Commission has had the advantage of being able to propose legislation as well as setting the agenda and holding important formal powers with regard to competition legislation. The Energy Directorate has attempted to build an energy policy agenda on the basis of this formal competence, especially within the internal market concept. It has also extended the IEM to other policy areas such as transport and state aid, and has sought to 'export' the IEM in the creation of an international regime for energy trade. Below we outline the policy content of this expansion and discuss its significance. In Chapter 4 we show how the Commission has expanded the energy policy agenda beyond the original IEM concept.

A competence for networks

The Commission has achieved some formal competence for itself in the area of infrastructure, which is arguably part of the IEM as it is a condition for transportation within a market.

Although the treaty revisions at Maastricht did not include a chapter on a common energy policy it did mandate an EU policy for the coordination and development of infrastructure, thus establishing an EU competence in this field. This treaty does not represent a new area of policy, rather it restates the objectives of the IEM: infrastructure must be developed for all of the EU region and beyond in order to enable the IEM to function – large parts of the EU are underdeveloped in terms of both gas and electricity networks, especially in the 'cohesion' countries in the south.

The new EU competence means that the Commission can decide which projects are most pressing and, through the cohesion funds it will have some funding to finance these projects. The amount available for trans-European networks in the period 1995–9 is 105 million ECUs, a much smaller amount than for other types of infrastructure. For the same period, road and rail have been awarded ECU1868 million ECUs and telecommunications 422 million ECUs. However the Commission considers that energy networks can attract private funding much more easily than roads so its funding will go towards feasibility studies, loan guarantees and interest rate subsidies.

The European Investment Bank has introduced a special 'window' for trans-European and other EU infrastructural projects, which may lead to increased lending to this sector. At the Essen European Council in December 1994 the first batch of trans-European networks was approved. Of the ten projects on the 'A list' five concerned electricity links, mainly in the south of Europe, and five concerned gas links in the south and from Algeria and Russia to the EU.

An obstacle to the energy networks is that there are still major differences between the transit, import and export regulations of the member countries. The commissioner for finances and the chairman of the trans-European network group of the Commission stressed the importance of this at the Essen summit: 'At the moment, we are trying to get free access [to networks]. The more free access you can achieve, the more profitable it will be to finance these networks.' This underlines the strategy of the Commission and also the very close connection between various areas of the IEM: without third party access there is little rationale for a full trans-European energy network, and without such a network the full potential of third party access cannot be realised.

It should be noted that the Commission works on several fronts simultaneously: while promoting the third party access issue in the working groups and in the normal decision-making fora, it also supports the need for third party access in attempting to launch new energy networks, utilising its newly acquired formal competence.

As might be expected, interest groups in the energy sector oppose this view of the relationship between networks and third party access: Eurogas, the association of the European gas industry, finds the whole trans-European concept unnecessary – networks should be developed on the basis of market principles, that is, if there is a demand, a network will be built. Hastily introducing a trans-European network will eradicate the 'level playing field', it is argued.

Policy on state aid

Not only is the existence of monopolies in the energy sector a problem from the point of view of the IEM, but state aid is also hard to monitor and evaluate. The Commission has granted aid for nuclear and other forms of renewable energy, and is developing a new aid policy, RECHAR II, for the restructuring of coal mining regions (*EER*, 29 July 1994). The 1994–97 programme is being financed by the structural funds and amounts to 400 million ECUs. RECHAR II replaces the first aid programme, which ran from 1989 to 1994.

The competition commissioner has noted that member state attitudes towards state aid have gradually converged with those of the Commission, as deregulation and privatisation are current policy trends in states that have hitherto extensively relied on state aids. The Competition Directorate has negotiated directly with national governments on aid, and states that its aim is 'to make policy predictable by laying down ground rules' (ibid., 25 November 1994, p. 5). Incidentally, this is what business and industry interest groups increasingly want too – in the form of a 'level playing field'. The directorate does a lot of work behind the scenes in preventing aid for plans that are not compatible with the treaty rules, allowing for the gradual phasing-out of aid in some cases. In most cases, notes the commissioner, 'national authorities are persuaded to amend initial plans which were unacceptable under the treaty' (ibid.)

The policy on state aid for the coal industry is of particular importance. Investment in the coal sector in Europe is undergoing a steady decline, and coal policy is increasingly focusing on employment and restructuring:

> In the future, investment will have to comply with the nationalisation, rationalisation and modernisation plans . . . under the new state aid system. This seeks to make the coal industry viable, while respecting the required cuts in the level of aid and its compliance with environmental protection provisions, and granting a proper amount of attention to the social and regional problems caused by the pit closures. (Ibid., 14 October 1994, p. 4)

As discussed in Chapter 1, EU coal can not compete with imported coal, and this will have to be reflected in the subsidies allowed by the Commission. The RECHAR programmes seek to smooth the transition from coal production to other industrial activity, but as we will see in Chapter 6, there is considerable disagreement between the Commission and Germany with regard to coal subsidies.

The IEM as a legal international regime

The Commission has also proposed an alternative route towards the IEM – the creation of an international regime that contains the IEM as its core philosophy:

The European Energy Charter is based on the IEM. In fact the charter can be read as an extension of the IEM to all of Europe and beyond, and Japan is one of the signatories. However the charter goes beyond the IEM, as will be discussed in Chapter 4.

A major part of the charter is devoted to ensuring that free market principles are also followed in the CIS and Central Europe. It started as a general process, but was gradually linked to existing trade regimes and rules, and now largely follows GATT rules and procedures (this process is analysed in detail by Andersen, 1996). In the initial stages, however, the process was dominated by the EU and the Commission.

The charter is not legally binding, but it is accompanied by a so-called basic agreement and a legally binding treaty, which was signed in December 1994. Accompanying protocols will be negotiated in the areas of environment and energy, hydrocarbons and nuclear safety. The aim of the charter is to promote an efficient energy market through the price mechanism, with due attention being paid to the environment (*Energy Monthly*, November 1991). The protection of investments is of particular importance, and the repatriation of profits will also have to be guaranteed.

IEM principles figure strongly in the charter and as such represent an extension of the IEM to a much larger geographical area than just the EU. The Commission's strategy for a major international energy charter is discussed in the following chapter, however it is important to note that here the need for a legal regime guaranteeing free market rules in Russia and Central Europe coincided with the Commission's work on the IEM. The Commission was thus in a very favourable position to draft a set of rules that would aid private investors in the East while also consolidating the case for free market rules in general in the energy sector. As stated, this sector is in many ways undergoing a 'paradigm shift', such that market principles are gradually replacing a strongly state-controlled sector reliant on subsidies and entrusted with public service functions. The Commission has promoted the IEM as a new paradigm both internally in the EU and as an international concept. The charter can be seen as an important part of this strategy.

The Euro-Mediterranean strategy

The Commission has also used the concept of a charter based on the principles of the IEM in its policy towards the Maghreb area. In 1995 it developed a 'Mediterranean strategy' – a plan of action for the agreement of association with these countries. In light of the political unrest in Algeria, which supplies the EU with 42 per cent of its natural gas requirements, this is very important for energy policy. There is, as stated earlier, great concern about security of supply to Europe, especially since the proportion of imports will rise. The political strategy here is a traditional EU response: creating economic interdependence as a means of achieving political stability.

At the Essen Summit in December 1994 it was decided to develop such a strategy not only eastwards but also towards the south. The energy directorate took the initiative in defining energy as the key to this strategy, and convened an interministerial meeting in Spain to hear the views of all parties. The proposal was to create some form of energy charter for the region. The Commission has sufficient financial instruments available to make this an attractive option for the Maghreb countries. The aim of the new charter is to extend the IEM to this region in order 'to encourage free trade, economic integration, and closer political and security cooperation' (*Energy Monthly*, April 1995, p. 8).

The Mediterranean strategy mirrors the strategy for Central Europe, which is discussed in the next chapter. In this context energy is an important instrument of linkage politics – it is important to secure energy supplies from the region, but it will also contribute to political stabilisation through economic interdependence. In the case of energy, such dependency will take in the physical form of oil and gas pipelines between North Africa and the Iberian peninsula and Italy.

The EU has a long history of attempting to create political stability through economic cooperation – this was really the principle idea of integration according to the 'founding fathers'. The implication for energy policy is that energy is seen as a prime instrument for such linkage politics, and energy is thus a major factor in building the agenda. The scope of the latter is being extended all the time under the umbrella of the IEM.

Free market rules for exploration and production

In May 1992, the Energy Directorate proposed that competition legislation be applied to the production of oil and gas. This meant that concession rules would have to be harmonised and that state-run companies would no longer enjoy a privileged position. However control over the rate of depletion and other resource management issues would remain with the member governments. The Commission's draft directive (COM92/110) also aimed at applying competition legislation to the granting of concessions. The intention was to ensure equal treatment, regardless of nationality, of applicants for exploration and production licenses for oil and gas, and to abolish the special national treatment that existed in Denmark and Norway (but no longer in Britain). The draft directive stated that concession policy should be 'non-discriminatory and transparent and impose no conditions on access to or exercise of those activities which are not technically warranted by the objective of optimum exploitation'. The contents of the directive were reflected in the final energy charter text, which established equal treatment for all applicants for exploration licenses, albeit with transition periods for some countries.

The directive was eventually adopted in a modified form, having been strongly supported by Britain but opposed by Denmark and the Netherlands.

Conclusions

The initial IEM proposals included a package of four proposals on the transportation of electricity and gas, as well as transparency of energy prices, as outlined by the Energy Directorate in autumn 1989. The gas and electricity directives were adopted in October 1990. The gas transportation directive, which had been rigorously and persistently opposed by gas transporters and producers, was adopted by majority voting, while the electricity directive was unanimously accepted. The directive on energy prices was modified before adoption, and the proposed 'clearing-house' for energy investments was not accepted due to British fears that it would result in further bureaucracy in Brussels.

In 1991 there was an additional proposal for third party access to gas pipelines and electricity grids, but not to the distribution networks. This proposal was described as 'very ambitious' by some in the Commission. The proposals on gas and electricity transportation could have been adopted by the Commission alone, but this would hardly have been realistic because they were politically very controversial.

The Commission's push towards the creation of an IEM has met with mixed success. Many of its controversial proposals have not been adopted, and those that have been adopted have been substantially diluted. The 1989 proposals on the transportation of gas and electricity, which marked the beginning of the process, were partially adopted in their original form: the electricity directive was adopted in more or less its original form, while the gas directive was modified to involve some 29 regional gas companies only, and was adopted by majority voting only after protracted negotiations.

The 1991 draft directive on third party access to electricity and gas has been the subject of rather unfruitful and long-drawn-out negotiations in working groups and the usual EU fora, and at the Energy Council meeting in June 1995 only some parts of the Commission's strategy were agreed to. The competition commissioner strongly denounced France's single buyer proposal, stressing that there was no reason why energy should be exempt from EU competition law. The IEM proposals 'in essence go no further than expressing existing rights in the treaty', he stated (*Energy Monthly*, 16 December 1994, p. 8). However the energy commissioner stressed that it was he who was responsible for energy policy, not the Competition Directorate, and that if the two proposals (third party access and single buyer), proved compatible, he could accept their coexistence.

Obviously there are strong disagreements about how to create an IEM, not only between the Commission, member governments and interest groups, but also between directorates.

In the mid 1980s, the EU played little part in energy policy, but ten years later energy companies and national politicians now look to Brussels in fear or anticipation of new proposals. This shift does not mean that the IEM will be adopted in the way the Commission wants it, but it does signal a major move away from nationally controlled energy policy towards the need for European-wide rules on deregulation and liberalisation.

4

Towards a Common Energy Policy?

Introduction: taking advantage of external 'windows of opportunity'

We turn now to energy policy proposals that go beyond the IEM to the formation of a common energy policy (CEP), whereby policy-making power would be transferred from the member states to the EU institutions, informally and/or formally.

The Commission has consistently taken advantage of external 'windows of opportunity' to launch CEP proposals. First, the crisis in the Middle East formed the background for a proposal by the Energy Directorate that it be responsible for a 60-day emergency oil stock for Community consumption, and that the Commission should not only decide when and how to use this oil (*EC Energy Monthly*, November 1990), but also that it should harmonise national oil price mechanisms since they 'threaten the free movement of goods within the EU in times of crisis'. The Commission even proposed to work towards abolishing the link between oil and gas prices, starting with negotiations with major gas sellers. Such a decoupling would encourage gas use when the price for oil was high, instead of vice versa, and thus made very good sense from the security of supply viewpoint, it was argued.

This proposal was strongly opposed by interest groups and member states. What is of major interest here, however, is the fact that the Commission proposed to intervene directly in the pricing mechanisms, both in terms of national policy and between energy carriers. In principle this represented a major deviation from the IEM concept, which was aimed at allowing commercial actors to compete more freely.

While the importance of promoting gas for security of supply and environmental reasons is fairly uncontroversial, an EU energy policy that would respond to these needs would imply new and more powerful policy instruments on the part of the Commission than those contained in the IEM proposals and this would involve the transfer of power to the EU from the nation state, something that certainly would be controversial. In addition, political intervention in the price mechanism for oil and/or gas by any standards would be regarded as strong political tool, and bound to meet heavy resistance on the part of commercial actors.

Second, the Commission proposed to apply for membership of the International Energy Agency (IEA). It wanted to be classified as a 'participating country' and to be entitled to vote *in place of the member states* on matters 'falling within its field of competence'. The one vote of the Commission would thus represent all the EU members. Little was said about which areas of competence should belong to the Commission and which to individual member states, but an indication was given in the statement that 'the Community is increasingly required to demonstrate its identity in relation to the rest of the world, including in the field of energy. It is important that the Community should now emulate its main industrialized partners, notably the US and Japan, and take its place as a key player in the international oil sector' (ibid., December 1990). The assertive tone here is noticeable.

The adoption of these proposals would have meant a more central role for the Commission in energy policy, and both were rejected in their original form by the Energy Council in May 1990. The idea of IEA membership was, however, not negatively received, but a clear demarcation line between the Commission's role and that of the member states was demanded by the latter. Both proposals had been 'hastily put together at the start of the Gulf crisis since Cardoso, then Energy Commissioner; saw the political opportunity a Gulf crisis might offer' and it was considered that the Commission 'was requesting sweeping powers' (ibid.)

The Commission was thus adept at utilising opportunities presented by external events, but was not very successful in achieving the agreement of member governments.

However the work towards the IEM underlined the need for a common energy policy in the sense that it implied decision-making power on the part of the EU institutions that as yet did not exist. The more controversial the Energy Directorate's proposals were, the more acute this need seemed to be. As argued above, the IEM would not be a Thatcherite 'rolling back of the state', but it does presuppose political reregulation. Those CEP proposals that reflected both general external political needs and 'internal logic' thus remained on the agenda and were partially adopted.

The CEP proposals

The three CEP proposals that will be analysed in detail here – a chapter in the Treaty on European Union on a legal basis for a CEP, the carbon tax proposal and the policy towards Central Europe – were all responses to external events but were also logical, given the move towards the IEM. The Commission designed these proposals in a way that seemed to take into account an external policy problem that was common to member governments, but built on the IEM logic and on the existing energy policy within the EU. It combined policy instruments to make up a comprehensive package for Central Europe that included energy as a major component, but as we shall see it did not manage to create such a package in the case of carbon tax. The most ambitious move was to try to establish a formal competence for a CEP in the Treaty on European Union.

The proposal for a separate chapter on energy in the treaty included the IEM, a policy for a community-wide system of supply security, the integration of energy and environmental policy and an 'external policy which enhances the Community's standing and influence on the world stage' (*EC Energy Monthly*, December 1990, p. 24). The turn of external events – primarily the energy–environmental crisis in Central Europe and the Gulf crisis – underlined the need for additional policy-making power in the energy field, according to the Commission. As the IEM developed further, the need for a coordinated security-of-supply policy became apparent.

In early 1995, in preparation for the intergovernmental conference in 1996, the Commission issued a document called the 'Green Paper on a CEP'. Here it stated there would be three pillars to the CEP: environmental considerations, security of supply, and the IEM principles. This was an attempt to achieve formal competence for a CEP in the treaty revision in 1996.

The Commission has repeatedly attempted to develop a common policy for security of supply, and this is one area where the IEM proposals clash with national priorities. Energy subsidies are a case in point. Often a member state will subsidise its domestic energy sources for social and labour policy reasons, but justifies this on grounds of supply security. Given the magnitude of this problem, the Commission envisages a long transitional period before an EU-wide outlook is established. It will start by invoking competition law to phase out national subsidies, and in the case of coal the RECHAR programme will assist in the task:

> The transition from national systems to ensure security of supply to a community energy system in the internal market will be accomplished in successive stages. The first stage consists of supporting national measures for aid, the harmonisation of existing practises and the convergence of national measures in favour of Community interests. The second phase will have to ensure the best possible exploitation of the existing interdependence and complementarity in the EU. This gradual approach will have to be implemented in parallel with a periodic review, every five years, of the EC's long-term energy objectives. (*Europe*, 11 July 1991)

Thus as early as 1990 several developments that together constituted major elements of a common energy policy were evident in the EU. Many perceived that concrete and far-reaching policy action was called for – as evidenced in the proposals outlined above – but that the Energy Directorate probably lacked most of the necessary policy instruments to implement energy policy in response to these events. This accelerated the attempt to create a more powerful directorate.

Some member governments signalled their approval of an EU-wide energy policy: Italy espoused this idea throughout its presidency in the autumn of 1990, and the Belgian Secretary of State for energy even envisaged EU-level management of all EU energy resources and networks. There appeared to be a general recognition of the limitations inherent in the IEM – concept. For instance, an effective security-of-supply policy for oil should include stocks that could be deployed as a countermeasure to increases in oil prices. Economies of scale were seen as an additional advantage of an EU-level energy policy (Interview, Brussels, 1990). Support was also forthcoming from the European Council and the president of the commission, Jacques

Delors, who regarded energy as a prime area of general European integration. Thus the view appeared to emerge that without a common energy policy, other areas of integration would not materialise.

The three major CEP developments are discussed in more detail below.

The fight for a formal competence

As stated above, the Commission tried to have a chapter inserted in the Treaty on European Union formalising a CEP competence. This was rejected by Britain, Germany and the Netherlands – all energy producers who feared that the EU would develop a supranational role if armed with such a competence.

The treaty amendment proposal contained four articles. The first stated that the EU was to have a 'common energy policy'. This was to be coordinated with the Euratom and ECSC treaties. Article 2 defined the contents of the CEP: it would guarantee security of supply in the EU, contribute to the stability of the energy market, continue the work towards the IEM, define and determine the measures to be taken for all energy sources in the event of a crisis, and ensure a high degree of environmental protection. In the third article it was laid down that energy policy should be arrived at by qualified majority voting, and in Article 4 that the internal market rules could be set aside in an emergency situation (*Europe*, 27 February 1991). Furthermore 'the Community shall contribute to the establishment and development of trans-European networks in the area . . . of energy infrastructures . . .' (TEU, para. 129). This follows the paragraphs on energy proper. At the Maastricht summit of the European Council in December 1991, however, the entire chapter was rejected. Since treaty amendments require unanimity, one opposing voice was enough for the proposal to fall.

Despite this setback, from 1991 energy and the need for a CEP loomed large in the Commission's work programmes. The argument was again that the work towards IEM demanded a larger political mandate for the Commission, for instance in the field of infrastructure, and aid to develop electricity and gas networks. The 1991 Commission work programme stated that, 'there will be moves to spell out the essential features of a CEP . . . in light of the lessons learned from the Gulf War, the Commission plans to develop the external facet of the a CEP . . . hand in hand with the very necessary development of cooperation in energy matters, taking the practical form of a pan-European energy charter'. Work on oil crisis management and environmentally friendly energy use was specifically mentioned. When Commission President Delors presented the work programme he specifically mentioned energy as the key integrative policy area between Eastern and Western Europe. He also indicated that the IEM must be accompanied by the development of a security-of-supply policy on the part of the Community (Commission Work Programme, 1991).

The quest for a formal CEP competence continued, and in early 1995 a Green Paper on the CEP set out the main features of such a policy. They included the furthering of the IEM, the development of a security-of-supply policy and the integration of environmental criteria into energy policy. However the Green Paper did not suggest a supranational role for the Commission, but suggested the need for a CEP that would be based on the interests of the member states. It also called for consultation and discussion, 'establishing confidence between member states via transparency, dialogue and exchange of information, guaranteeing convergence within diversity' (*EC Energy Monthly*, 13 January 1995).

This time the Commission was proceeding very cautiously indeed: it clearly wanted to obtain a consensus on the need for a CEP through open discussion, being fully aware of the fact that a CEP competence in the treaty could only be adopted if the decision was unanimous. In the Green Paper there was no definition of a new role for the Commission, but rather a focus on the need for an energy policy in Europe: 'Whatever the energy resources of each member state, whatever their respective energy balance, the Community as a whole has to respond to the challenges of industrial competitiveness, security of supply and environmental protection.' The Commission invited all interested parties to form a 'common vision' for energy policy over the next twenty years, centring on the necessity of reconciling the need for competition in the energy markets with the demands of the environment and security of supply. The paper analysed these problems and concluded that 'the coherent development of policy instruments is hindered because of the absence of clear responsibilities for energy policy at the Community level'.

In sum the Green Paper made a careful start on a comprehensive approach to the topic of a CEP, concentrating on policy needs instead of discussing who would be responsible for what in terms of policy-making. This was probably a wise approach given the opposition of many member states to a major role for the EU in energy policy.

Work on the proposed new chapter on a CEP, to be discussed along with other treaty amendments at the intergovernmental conference in 1996, started in 1994. Both the Economic and Social Committee and the European Parliament drafted such a chapter, but while the former wanted unanimous decision-making, the latter recommended qualified majority voting in its proposal for a CEP chapter, and also stressed the environmental dimension. A few member governments – the 'cohesion' countries, Italy and Belgium – strongly favour a formal CEP competence. France is opposed to the idea and considers that the EU should have some role in coordinating policy but that energy policy for the various energy types must be left to the member states. The other member states are rather hostile to the Commission's attempts to create a CEP (ibid., June 1995, p. 9). The energy producers are wary of losing their national autonomy and also of any energy policy developments that go beyond the IEM.

The real fear of many interest groups as well as of member states is that the Commission will develop policies that favour some energy types over others – as is in fact envisaged in the environment articles in the Treaty on European Union, discussed later in this chapter. If the environmental implications of energy policy are taken into account, then 'dirty' energy use cannot be treated neutrally. Whatever the policy instrument – taxes or subsidies – clean energy use must be promoted. This inevitably means that coal and oil will be disadvantaged. This will involve intense political battles over substance and principle, and is contrary to the IEM which simply tries to harmonise regulation of the energy market. Many energy actors fear that the Commission will try to use its proposed CEP competence to develop policy that goes beyond the IEM: 'It is not at all clear yet what such a policy would contain . . . a fear of the energy industry and some member state governments is that DGXVII [the Energy Directorate] may try to influence what fuel sources should be used . . . some observers believe that pushing energy policy up the agenda has everything to do with internal Commission politics, and the need for DGXVII to justify its future existence' (ibid., 15 August 1994, p. 5). This was a common interpretation in Brussels. The environmental NGOs are however calling for CEP powers in order to create an environmentally friendly energy policy. These include all the major groups federated in the European Environmental Bureau.

The process of gaining support for the CEP is being carefully handled by the Commission. It consults very widely with all potential interest groups, but 'to date, the industry response has tended to be suspicious' (*EC Energy Monthly*, 15 August 1994, p. 5). The Commission argues that consumers should welcome a CEP because it will offer the best guarantee of an effective overall energy policy through the harmonisation of different energy policy goals at the European level. According to a representative of the Energy Directorate, 'We should tell them that if they have not got an effective energy policy they should not be surprised if their competitive position is poor, they have environmental tensions and their relations with non-energy producer countries differ' (*EER*, 14 October 1994).

The schedule for the CEP was that the Commission should sound out the views of the member states in a process that would last until the end of the 1995. This was very important since the Commission's eventual CEP chapter can fall by the veto of just one government and the Commission wants to avoid being defeated once more on this issue. Therefore it is trying to convince the member states that the idea of a CEP has been theirs all along, drawing on the 'wish list' for energy that the states themselves have made. It is also argued that the potential security-of-supply problem of gas to the EU, which depends on Algeria and Russia for two thirds of its gas imports, has made a CEP competence an urgent issue (*EC Energy Monthly*, 15 February 1994, p. 4). There is no doubt that external events will aid the Commission in setting an agenda for energy policy – the problem of supply security for gas will not disappear in the near future.

Even though there has been little support among the member governments for an energy policy competence in the new treaty the Commission does not regard it has lost the battle. It has continued to argue the need for a formal competence, but only on a par with that in other policy areas, for instance the environment (EU, White Paper, 1996). It has been careful not to propose an enhanced role for itself, but instead stresses that it should coordinate member states' policies to the extent that this is logical.

The environment and energy policy

The other important driving force towards a CEP is the ascendance of environmental issues on the international agenda. The need to establish an environmentally sound energy policy came to the fore in the EU during 1990. In May 1990 the Energy Council called for energy saving, the incorporation of environmental concerns into future energy policy and further debate on the role of nuclear energy.

Environmental policy has a rather short history in the EU. There have been several 'action programmes' since 1973, the first three of which contained no specific proposals for change. However the fourth programme, which ran from 1987 until 1992, was comprehensive. A new programme was published in March 1992 covering the period until year 2000. It stressed the need to improve the policy instruments that the EU has in the environmental field, and the need to use fiscal instruments: environmental costs should be added to the price of services and goods, and the concept of sustainable development operationalised (COM23/92).

The Single European Act introduced the environment as an area of EU policy and was duly added to the Treaty of Rome. Paragraphs 130r, s and t stress prevention and polluters should pay for damage they cause ('the polluter pays principle'). The environment includes the quality of the physical environment as well as any adverse effects on people's health, and each step towards the internal market must be accompanied by analysis of the consequences this will have for the environment. The environment is not limited to the EU geographical area, and the EU may impose environmental standards outside its boundaries and act on behalf of other regions (Haigh and Baldock, 1989; Wilkinson, 1992). Environmental standards are already tied to much of the financial aid given to Central Europe (interview, EBRD, London, 1992).

In the Treaty on European Union the inclusion of the environment in EU policy-making was furthered in several ways. First, it was stipulated that the EU would 'promote economic and social progress which is balanced and sustainable' (Article B, TEU). In Article 130r the obligation on the part of the EU to 'promote measures at the international level' is specifically mentioned. Decision-making procedures were also amended: Article 130s states that unanimity is required for (1) fiscal proposals such as a carbon tax, (2) proposals that affect land use and resource management, and (3) 'measures *significantly affecting a member state's choice between different energy resources and the general structure of its energy supply*' (emphasis added). However it is the Council that decides whether any of the proposals listed above will form part of the internal market, and thus they are subject to majority voting.

Second, qualified majority voting is the procedure for all legislation in Paragraph 130r, which includes 'preserving, protecting and improving the quality of the environment; protecting human health, prudent and rational utilization of natural resources, and measures at the international level'.

Third, a new decision-making procedure has been introduced – the co-determination procedure. This is to be applied to environmental legislation (including the action programmes) in all areas but the three listed above. The codetermination procedure allots a larger role to the European Parliament than allowed for in the cooperation procedure the main decision-making mode which is based on majority voting and which was adopted in the SEA. Matters of a fiscal nature and those with a direct bearing on the energy policy of member states will remain subject to unanimous voting.

The decision-making procedures in environmental policy are important in their implications for energy policy. The Treaty on European Union envisages an environmental policy that encourages certain energy forms over others. Decisions for such a policy are to be taken unanimously. However qualified majority voting will apply to all other environmental legislation. Thus it may be inferred that, to the extent that environmental policy includes energy issues, energy policy has already received an indirect legal basis in the treaty.

But when it comes to the actual integration of energy and environmental policy there are few common policy proposals. A sensitive energy issue with clear environmental implications is that of subsidised coal production. As yet environmental concerns have not been tied explicitly to coal production, although the reduction of coal production will be hastened by the strategies to reduce CO_2 emissions. The Commission determines whether coal production should be subsidised in member countries, based on the rules laid down in the Treaty of Rome and the ECSC treaty. In the future coal production and use may be linked to environmental issues as the Energy Directorate has indicated that it will support the enhanced use of natural gas and nuclear energy for power generation. Coal may thus be deemphasised in future energy policy, and the environmental pressure to curtail industrial emissions will undoubtedly give impetus to the running down of coal subsidies.

The carbon tax

The most controversial issue involving energy and environmental policy in the EU is the carbon tax proposal, which has lingered on the agenda for many years. An expert group report on the environmental effects of the internal market stated very clearly that increased economic growth will result in a correspondingly higher level of pollution, and that environmental measures must therefore be comprehensively integrated with the internal market project. This became a major theme in EU policy: 'Taxing pollution, not only for environmental reasons but also to generate revenue to reduce labour costs and boost employment, is one of Jacques Delors' favourite themes' (*EER*, 9 December 1994, p. 7). He introduced this in the final chapter of the 'White Paper on Growth, Competitiveness, and Employment' (1994), and eco-taxes are now a major issue in the economic policy discussions in the Commission.

In a communication adopted by the Commission in November 1994 entitled 'Economic Growth and the Environment' (COM465/94), the commissioner for economic affairs argued for the use of economic instruments as the best tool for integrating environmental policy into sectoral policies, and that environmental taxes were the best way to do this. This in itself was not a new idea, but the fact that the commissioner for economic affairs launched the proposal shows that it was within the mainstream of EU policy thinking, and as such had the general backing of the Commission.

In 1990 a carbon tax had been proposed by the environment commissioner as a way of imposing a penalty for energy use. The tax proposal was aimed at meeting the Community goal of stabilising the CO_2 emission levels agreed in late 1990 by the year 2000, and the proposed energy tax would reflect the thermal content of the fuel, which varies with carbon content. The tax would exempt primary use fuels and renewables and was envisaged to be approximately $10 barrel of oil. Tax income would be used to promote environmentally friendly energy use. The Commission further proposed working actively with the gas industry to promote 'least cost planning' and better procedures for the production and distribution of gas and electricity within the EU.

Several policy options for reducing carbon emissions were discussed at the energy–environmental meeting in December 1990. June 1991 was set as the deadline for specific action on how to implement a carbon tax. During the run-up to the UN Conference on Environment and Development (UNCED) in 1992, the carbon tax proposal took on increased importance in EU discussions. However in the Energy and Environment Council meeting in December 1991 the tax was accepted in principle only, with the adoption of the 'Community Strategy to Limit CO_2 Emissions and to Improve Energy Efficiency'. The Council asked the Commission to prepare the text for a directive on such a tax, however it also required studies of the macroeconomic and policy consequences, the consequences for energy-intensive industry, how the lesser-developed EU members would be able to modify the tax and so on. In addition all member states were required to submit details of their national programmes for emission abatement. Thus many aspects of the carbon tax had to be resolved before the Council would give its approval and a new deadline for a common position was set for the end of April 1992, in view of the forthcoming international environmental negotiations. The December Council meeting also stressed the importance of the view of the finance ministers in this matter.

There was opposition to the carbon tax – which it was finally decided would be a carbon/energy tax, split 50–50 between carbon content and energy use – both inside and outside the EU decision-making structure. Lobbies at the national level in the coal, oil and oil-related sectors opposed the tax and put pressure on their national governments. Within the EU, the Advisory Committee of the European Coal and Steel Community questioned the need for a carbon tax as such, arguing that a global regime for all emissions was needed. The Commission replied that the objection that the EU must not act alone was a prime concern. Very hostile reactions to the tax were voiced in the Gulf Cooperation Council, consisting of Commission representatives and members of OPEC. It was maintained that such a tax would have a direct effect on the interests of the oil producers.

Doubts about agreement being reached before the UNCED conference seemed to increase, although the official stance was that a position would be reached. The energy commissioner expressed the view that unilateral acceptance of a tax could undermine competitiveness, a concern shared by other representatives of the Energy Directorate. However the environment commissioner denied that he shared this view and stressed that unilateral EU action would allow pressure to be brought to bear on the US and Japan. He also said that the Commission would 'soon' change the communication on this issue into a draft directive.

As this was the province of both directorates the energy commissioner had to agree to the proposed directive, which required both
ministers to reach a unanimous common position. The internal
struggle between those who favoured a tax and those who wanted
to wait until after the Rio conference was increasing, and a conflict
between the Energy and Environment Directorates was apparent.

The Energy and Environment Council made acceptance of the tax
conditional on multilateral action. In a Council meeting in May 1992
it was emphasised that the EU could only accept such a tax if the US
and Japan followed suit. The question of competitiveness was para-
mount here. As a consequence of this decision Environment Commissioner Ripa di Meana did not participate in the Rio conference, and
the EU did not succeed in playing a leading role there. The climate
policy eventually adopted consisted of programmes for energy saving
and renewable fuels, but the important carbon tax was lacking.

The saga of the carbon tax continued throughout 1995 and 1996.
Britain vetoed the tax each time it appeared on the Council's agenda,
not so much for energy policy reasons as for reasons of principle: it
was simply not acceptable that the EU should levy taxes.

Meanwhile it was becoming increasingly clear that the EU could
not meet its CO_2 reduction targets through the proposed policy
measures, including the tax and national-level measures. During
the German EU presidency in 1994 there was an attempt to revive
the tax proposal by including it in an existing directive on excise
duties for mineral oils. The idea was to avoid the British veto by
simply increasing the tax on oil use and attributing part of the
existing taxes to environmental causes. However the problem here
is that CO_2 emissions stem from the burning of other fossil fuels as
well, especially coal and natural gas. Furthermore, unlike in the
original proposal there would be no component of the tax aimed at
restricting general energy use, thus energy saving would not be one of
the effects of the tax. An improved version of this was a draft directive
to extend the taxes on oil to natural gas and coal. When this proposal
was discussed at the Environment Council in Dresden in late 1994,
and later in the same year at the European Council in Essen, Britain
once more rejected any Community-level strategy to combat CO_2
emissions, even if it was 'dressed up' as an existing excise duty (*EER*,
29 July 1994).

The French, who took over the presidency in January 1995,
pleaded for the policy work to continue, but after the Essen European
Council in December 1994 the issue was a dead one, at least in the

form of a common tax. The Council stated that the ministers 'have taken note of the Commission's intention of submitting guidelines to enable every member state to apply a CO_2/energy tax on the basis of common parameters *if it so desires*' (*EC Energy Monthly*, 16 December 1994, p. 11). In other words the EU would not impose a common tax but would attempt to develop common guidelines for such a tax for those member states that wanted one. However the tax continues to be on the agenda as Belgium and the Netherlands favour a tax with an 'opt-out clause'. The Commission has not formally withdrawn the tax proposal, but has modified it along these lines. Yet there appears to be little prospect for a common tax.

Energy policy towards Central Europe and the CIS

The acute need for more and cleaner energy in Central Europe has served to accelerate the merging of energy and environmental policy and the development towards a stronger degree of common energy policy. The Commission has consistently tried to link energy and the environment in forging its policy towards prospective EU members in the region.

The EU has several formal political ties to the region. For example the European Bank for Reconstruction and Development (EBRD) was established to provide aid for economic development. Situated in London, the bank started its work in April 1991. The underwriting countries include the US and non-EU countries in Europe. The European Investment Bank (EIB) provides loans to the energy sector and favours projects that are environmentally sound. As of 1991 it was authorised to lend to Poland and Hungary as well as in the former East Germany. A loan of 50 million ECUs was granted to Poland to enable it to modernise its gas industry. The money is earmarked for desulphurising Polish natural gas, thus contributing to a cleaner environment. In 1991, 93 per cent of its loans went to energy-related projects.

Both the CIS and the Central European countries are members of the European Environmental Agency (EEA), an EU institution founded in 1990. The negotiations between these countries and the EU, which started in October 1990, concluded with association agreements in December 1991, and it is the expressed aim of the former countries to participate fully in all EU environmental programmes.

The EU has funded two programmes that *inter alia* deal with environmental protection and energy in Hungary and Poland in addition to cofunding the Regional Environmental Centre, in Budapest. These programmes focus on improving air and water quality in the two countries. The PHARE programme, an EU programme designed to assist the economic restructuring of Central Europe, 'gave overwhelming priority to projects related to environmental protection'. In 1990 alone 3.5 million ECUs were paid out for environmental measures in Poland and Hungary.

The 'Group of 24', consisting of the EU and other OECD countries, also deal with energy and environmental problems in Central Europe. The Commission, which coordinates the work of this group, proposed that energy financing should become a priority in light of the double stress under which these countries were operating – the demand on the part of the CIS for energy payments in hard currency, and the Gulf crisis, which threatened to cause an increase in the price of oil. The Commission stressed the need for a pan-European medium-term energy strategy, proposing that all financial instruments be coordinated, that help be given to Central Europe to reduce its dependence on Russian energy, and that assistance in developing alternative gas import sources be provided. Importantly, gas use should be encouraged by technical and financial means. The development of the gas grid should be funded by the EU as the change to gas would contribute to environmental improvement.

The Group of 24's reception of the Commission's proposal was mixed, and no immediate measures were taken. However the importance here lies in the nature of the Commission's proposals. There is an indication that the Commission wants to take on the responsibility for coordinating and developing a fully-fledged strategy in the energy–environmental area, not only for its members, but specifically for the Central European region. In terms of financial policy instruments, the EIB and the EBRD are already in place. In its support to Central Europe the EIB looks at the environmental soundness of projects, and the EBRD prioritises the funding of projects that improve the environment. An 'environmental reflex' must be incorporated from the start, according to the Commission.

Energy plays a pivotal role in the EU's relationship with Eastern Europe, both in terms of the development of energy infrastructure, the funding of energy-efficient projects, and the charter.

Following the so-called 'Europe' agreements between the EU and the Visegrad countries (Hungary, Poland, the Czech Republic and

Slovakia), the latter are obliged to adapt to the EU's policies. As of October 1994 the heads of state and ministers from these countries began to participate in meetings with their EU counterparts, and a task force was established to harmonise legislation and policies. In the first interministerial meeting of foreign ministers on 31 October, 1994 the role of the environment was stressed: 'All sides underlined the importance of harmonising standards throughout the region and converging national policies. The need to take into account the EU's 5th Environmental Action Programme was also noted' (*Euro-East*, 14 November 1994).

At the Essen summit of the European Council in December 1994, to which the foreign ministers of the Visegrad countries were invited, a comprehensive strategy was agreed for the adaptations the Visegrad-countries, Bulgaria and Romania will have to make if they are to become EU members. as well as regular consultations between heads of state, ministers in most policy areas will meet to ensure that their new policies harmonise with those of the EU. Funding for a five-year programme to finance political and legal adaptation in all major policy fields was passed. The annual amount available for this purpose is about 1.1 billion ECUs. Further funding has been provided for infrastructural developments, including energy, as well as 3.5 million ECUs under the PHARE programme for the harmonisation of environmental law and policy.

International organisations such as the World Bank and the IMF are dealing with economic restructuring in Central Europe, but the EU's role is more comprehensive in that it is also seeking to aid political transformation. Conditions for EU membership are of both a political and an economic nature, tied to the criteria of a market economy and democracy. However the use of energy as a key to adaptation has also been prominent.

The energy charter

The most comprehensive plan for improving energy infrastructure and securing energy supply is the Energy Charter, which concerns the production and transportation of gas, especially that from the CIS. Introduced to the European Council in June 1990 by then Dutch Premier Ruud Lubbers, it was debated within the fora of the EU as well as in high-level meetings between the CIS and the EU.

The 'Lubbers Plan', as it was initially called, formed the basis for the deliberations between the Commission and Russia over energy supplies, especially gas from the CIS. The oil price volatility caused by the Gulf crisis and the concomitant Russian demand for energy payments in hard currency served to intensify the EU's work towards such a grand strategy. Because the Russian energy production system was in a state of crisis and the energy supply situation and the ability to pay for energy in Central Europe were in an equal state of emergency, only fairly swift action on the part of the EU, or coordinated by the EU, could hope to prevent a dangerous deterioration of the situation. At stake was not primarily the issue of energy itself, but the political stability of both the CIS and the Central European countries, as was repeatedly stressed by Jacques Delors.

The talks on the proposal for the energy charter that were held between Delors, Commissioners Andriessen and Cardoso e Cunha. The Russian vice prime minister showed a very open-minded attitude towards the introduction of Western market conditions for joint ventures in the energy sector. This high-level group concluded that the EU must assist Russia to produce and transport natural gas, in return for which the EU would receive a stable supply. The problems involved in this gigantic undertaking were reported to be 'technical and technological' only. The EU stressed its commitment to assist the Russian reforms but also that IEM rules would be part of the Energy Charter, as well as commercial conditions for Western companies with regard to the expatriation of profits, conditions for investments and so on.

The European Council mandated the Commission to progress with the charter at its December meeting in 1990, and adopting a draft communication outlining its contents. The rules of the charter reflected the IEM concept in general; that is, to establish commercial, binding rules for the transportation and sale of energy. Yet in order to cover exploration and production in joint ventures, these rules would have to go beyond the IEM concept. In a communication the energy commissioner stressed that concession rules would be part of the charter. Furthermore the charter would be binding, and therefore an administrative and coercive authority had to be established to survey and enforce the rules. This logically called for extended policy instruments on the part of the Commission.

The next step in the work towards the charter was a conference in autumn 1991, to which all European countries were invited. In spite of the political unrest in the then Soviet Union, the Commission did not postpone any of its general work on the Energy Charter, but rather intensified it. The European Parliament withdrew food aid on political grounds in early January, and the Commission postponed the joint EU–Russia meeting on economic–political cooperation scheduled for late January 1991. However this did not affect the progress towards the charter. In fact, as the EU had postponed the general bilateral talks because of the situation, cooperation in energy became even more important as one of the remaining links.

In December 1991 the charter was signed by all EU members, the EFTA members, the Central European states, the CIS, Japan and the US. The charter was not legally binding, but a so-called 'basic agreement' was being negotiated with the aim of creating a legally binding framework for the charter. The proposal for the basic agreement was presented by the Commission in April 1992, and in December 1994 the legally binding charter treaty was signed in Lisbon by approximately 50 countries.

The charter policy process was conducted by the EU alone, although there was talk of making it an IEA or a CSCE (Conference on Security and Cooperation in Europe, later OCSE) process. The Commission coordinated the policy process with the CSCE. At the CSCE summit in Paris in November 1991 Jacques Delors recommended the charter proposal as the best way of achieving East–West European integration, stating that 'une charte européenne de l'énergie pourrait créer un climat de confiance propice a l'utilisation optimale des ressources . . . et a une réduction des tensions et des équilibres dans la communauté internationale' (intervention by J. Delors).

The place of the charter process in EU energy policy, as seen by the Commission, was underlined in a communication from the latter to the CSCE conference in Helsinki, which started in late March 1992. Here the role of the two organisations was delineated by the Commission which stated that the Charter was a follow-up of a CSCE recommendation in the energy field, and that to *avoid duplication, no new initiatives* need be taken in Helsinki. However, the CSCE should support the charter it added.

The treaty stipulates that energy trade should be governed by GATT rules, and that exploration, production and transportation policy should be non-discriminatory. All signatories must allow the transit of energy from third parties, and must not disrupt this in the event of a conflict with one of the parties. This article is of major importance in view of the fact that Russian gas is transported via Ukraine and other republics where the potential for conflict with Russia exists. Investors will have their investments protected, while the host country is obliged to treat foreign and national companies in exactly the same way, although some countries are exempt from this rule during the pre-investment and transition phases.

Two institutions have been established to manage the treaty: the Charter Conference, which consists of the signatories and meets periodically, and the Charter Secretariat. The former is the decison-making body, and the Charter Secretariat is entrusted by with day-to-day management. The Secretariat was located in the Energy Directorate until a permanent site in Brussels was decided on in 1995. The Secretariat consists of a secretary-general, appointed by the charter conference, plus support staff. According to the Commission the Secretariat 'will remain small but could conceivably subcontract a part of its work to existing institutions' (*EER*, 25 November 1994, p. 8). It can be assumed that the relevant institution will be the Energy Directorate, although dispute settlements will be carried out through the GATT dispute settlement mechanisms.

The problem of nuclear energy in Eastern Europe

The Commission has also attempted to develop a policy for nuclear energy in Eastern Europe. The old Soviet-type reactors are a major headache for Western Europe. Until the opening of Central Europe and the demise of the Soviet Union very little was known about the state of the nuclear sector, but now a number of operational reactors have been identified that pose certain dangers and at least three nuclear plants have been deemed dangerous by the International Atomic Energy Agency: Chernobyl in Ukraine, Kozludoy in Bulgaria and Bohunice in Slovakia. The problem that faces the West – and the EU in particular as the major coordinator of policy for the area – is twofold: (1) it will be extremely costly to upgrade or shut down these plants, and (2) if they are shut down, how will the shortfall in energy be met? The plants in question supply a large proportion of the energy requirement of each of the states concerned and there is no obvious alternative source of supply. Furthermore their closure could pose a threat to gas supplies to the EU because there will be a much greater need for Russian gas for domestic use. This implies that the reactors should be upgraded rather than shut down. There is a need to improve the first-generation pressurised water reactors, the VVER 230s and the 11 operating Chernobyl RBMK design reactors.

The danger of a nuclear accident in Eastern Europe is real, and yet the West's response has been fairly passive because of the vast sums of money involved. A member of the energy committee of the European Parliament expressed his distress about this during a private conversation, saying that the EU is doing something about energy in Eastern Europe but is shying away from tackling the real issue, that of the nuclear industry (interview, EP, 1992).

What has the EU done so far? While there is still no fully-fledged nuclear policy towards Eastern Europe, the EU did coordinate the offer from the G-7 summit in Milan in July 1994 for $200 million in an initial grant to Chernobyl, followed up by loans from international institutions such as the World Bank and the EBRD. In addition the EU offered 500 million ECUs, 100 million ECUs of which was a grant from the TACIS programme and the rest a Euratom loan. The West demanded that Ukraine immediately shut down two of the three at Chernobyl and upgrade the rest, and also that it should restructure its energy sector by imposing market prices for energy. In addition, three reactors that were under construction should be upgraded to Western safety standards (*EC Energy Monthly*, 19 July 1994, p. 8). However Ukraine considered that much more money would be needed: 'If there is not enough money', said the chairman of Chernobyl, 'we [will] freeze the process of improving safety' (ibid., 15 August 1994, p. 10). However this was widely perceived in the West as an attempt at blackmail, and when the EU responded by saying it would withhold further EU assistance and negotiations over a global EU–Ukraine policy, Ukraine relented. In the summer of 1994 Ukraine accepted the Western demand to close Chernobyl. Nonetheless the negotiations continued until 1996, when an agreement on the closure of two of the four reactors in Chernobyl was finally reached.

Conclusions

The Commission has used the opportunities presented by the progress towards the IEM to pursue aspects of energy policy that have been on the agenda for a long time: security of supply for oil and gas, energy-related environmental policy and the extension of the IEM principles to other energy policy areas. The opening up of Eastern Europe led to the discovery of major energy and environmental problems in the region, and there was a clear policy vacuum in this respect. There was a need for an international actor to forge a comprehensive policy towards Eastern Europe, and the EU was the logical choice. Thus new windows of opportunity were opened in this period, and the logic behind the IEM provided a basis for agenda-building

However the Commission's desire for a common energy policy was not warmly received, and only a few of its proposals seemed to have a possibility of success. Its attempt to achieve a formal competence in the Treaty on European Union for a common energy policy was met with much opposition, as was the proposal for a carbon tax. Nonetheless the development of the Energy Charter was successful and provided the Commission with a new institutional role for itself.

A CEP has been central to the ambition of the Commission for a long time, but it was only with the advent of the IEM and several externally prompted opportunities to construct new policy that it was able to develop the concept. There is still no formal competence for a CEP and little likelihood of one being created, but there are various ways in which the EU can develop CEP policies using existing procedures and rules, as long as the member states agree.

Several of the CEP proposals were based on the IEM, and can be seen as logical extensions of the latter. Hence there is not always a clear distinction between the two.

5

The Role of Member Governments and Interest Groups

Governments and the internal energy market

How have the EU member governments responded to the idea of an internal energy market? In Chapter 2 we discussed the energy interests and policies of the major governments. In this chapter we will look at how these governments have acted in the EU policy-making process. We have chosen to emphasise the roles of four major governments, but will also include other states when relevant. All the governments have their own energy interests to protect, for example the exportation of nuclear-generated electricity is of great importance to France, whereas in Germany the coal sector is placing a constraint on the government.

The following is an overview of the reaction of various member governments towards the IEM.

Germany

Two major issues have dominated the German attitude towards the IEM: the third party access proposals for gas, and competition policy as it impacts on the coal sector. The gas transmission companies have been very active in their opposition to any change in the conditions for gas transmission, and have opposed the directive on gas transmission from the beginning. The German government has followed suit in this opposition. Both the gas industry and the Ministry of

Economics, which is in charge of much of German energy policy, have voiced strong reactions against the directive, and the German government voted against it, along with the Netherlands, in the Council of Ministers despite the many efforts to modify the proposal (*EC Energy Monthly*, 7 August 1988; *International Gas Report*, 2 September 1988). Apart from voicing the interests of its gas industry, the government feared that a new and unnecessary bureaucracy would be developed to administer the common carriage regulation. In this concern they echoed the traditional British attitude towards the EU. However some domestic interest groups did favour third party access. The 'Kronenberger Kreis', an influential group of industrialists and business people, issued a memorandum stating their opposition to all constraints on a free energy market, including the transmission monopoly and domestic coal subsidies (*International Gas Report*, 17 March 1989).

Turning to the case of coal production subsidies, we have already seen that this is a matter of policy-making between social partners. The *Jahrhundertvertrag* and *Hüttenvertrag* are political agreements of major importance to German social and labour relations. Until the internal market was launched there was no EU intervention in this aspect of German politics despite the fact that the Treaty of Rome contains explicit rules forbidding practises that distort competition. However, as the internal market developed intervention in the subsidisation of German coal become a very important to the Commission. The *Jahrhundertvertrag* regulates 55 per cent of total German coal production, and since the domestic electricity industry is obliged to use German coal, this contract violates free trade principles in the field of electricity.

Consumers pay a tax on their electricity bills – the *Kohlenpfennig* – which is illegal under EU law, although it was accepted by the EU in 1987 and 1988. However the Commission instructed that coal subsidies should be phased out to make them compatible with EU competition policy; if not, coal aid after 1988 would not be approved. There is some evidence that the German government welcomed the EU intervention in the case of coal subsidies: 'It will be very convenient for the German government to pass the buck to Brussels for cuts in the mining industry' (*EC Energy Monthly*, 4 August 1989). Another observer makes a similar point: 'Compulsion from Brussels served as an alibi for the Bonn government and was not unwelcome. Bonn exploited its domestic differences in its dealings with the Commission' (Padgett, 1992, p. 65).

Gradually the German government came to accept the Commission's demands, and as a consequence the Ruhr miners went on wildcat strikes and the coal mining companies protested vigorously. When the coal interests took the Commission to the European Court of Justice to contest its invalidation of the *Jahrhundertvertrag*, the government only reluctantly supported them and stated that its support was 'purely formal' (ibid., 9 April 1989, 11 September 1989, 5 October 1989). The government cooperated well with Brussels, so well that the latter sanctioned the *Jahrhundertvertrag* until 1991 and agreed to review the *Kohlenpfenning* only in 1993. In turn the German government stated that only when the negotiations proved impossible would it support the court case. The argument was that the coal subsidies could be justified on grounds of security of supply (ibid., 6 May 1989). However it was the German Constitutional Court that resolved this issue by declaring the *Kohlenpfennig* illegal in a ruling in December 1994. For the Commission, this was part of its general attack on state subsidies in the coal sector (ibid., 10 May 1989). The German government at first proposed that both subsidies and production be cut back further than agreed in the *Jahrhundertvertrag*, but this was deemed insufficient (*Energy in Europe*, 3 November 1989).

Apart from the case of coal and gas transmission, the government has favoured some IEM proposals, and while the German energy industry has disagreed with some of the proposals (for example third party access to gas) all in all it has favoured a freer market (*EC Energy Monthly*, August 1989). During 1992 there was a move towards conditional support for third party access, especially in the CDU/CSU parliamentary groups (ibid., April 1992). The oil industry faced few changes as a result of the IEM, and as far as environmental issues were concerned, Germany's standards were already stricter than most EU rules.

Since to a great extent the domestic energy sector in Germany is governed by free market rules (apart from coal and nuclear energy) the IEM proposals have not generated significant opposition. But in those areas where domestic interest groups have been very active (coal subsidies and third party access to gas) the government has been reluctant to support the EU proposals. This indicates that domestic interest groups have been important in determining of the government's position, although it has attempted to adapt to the IEM rules for the coal sector. This has been done by arguing that the EU rules will apply sooner or later and will thus invalidate domestic arrangements such as the *Jahrhundertvertrag*. However this strategy has been only partly successful as the government appears to be under strong pressure from domestic interest groups.

France

The French government has always had a strong hand in energy policy as the energy companies are state-owned. However even in France there has been some degree of privatisation. In general the French government has supported all the IEM developments except third party access to electricity. It has supported the EU policies against strong interest group opposition, for example when Gaz de France protested strenuously about third party access to gas. It should be added that the domestic position of Gaz de France is rather weak compared with that of Électricité de France, with which the government has sided in the work towards a freer electricity market. Due to the liberalisation of the electricity market under the IEM, French electricity exports increased by as much as 25 per cent in 1988–89. New export contracts have been signed with Portugal, Spain, Switzerland, Britain and Germany, countries which until recently have been obliged to use domestically produced coal for their electricity generation. The reduction of coal subsidies is thus closely related to the integration of Europe's electricity markets.

The French government has, however, gone beyond the EU context to further its electricity interests. At a summit meeting with Chancellor Kohl in 1989, President Mitterrand gave his support for German reunification in return for Germany's pledge to accept the EU coal subsidy rules as of 1993 and to cooperate in electricity trade. The protocol from the meeting includes steps on how to cooperate in the fields of energy efficiency, R&D in energy, oil and gas, and stipulates that the countries 'will invite the two [national] electricity companies to pursue their dialogues with deepening cooperation' (*Energy in Europe*, November 1989). Clearly the benefactor from this agreement in terms of energy will be France, which had thus built a commercial relationship through a high-level bilateral political agreement.

Prior to this agreement there had often been open hostility between French and German policy-makers in the EU regarding energy policy, and the German officials had accused the French of being overly active in using the IEM to their advantage. For example the

Jahrhundertvertrag had been acceptable to the Commission until as late as 1983–84, but after work on the internal market had got under way the Commission had started to enforce competition legislation. The Germans had then accused the French of being overzealous in reminding the Commission of the German coal subsidies (Padgett, 1992, p. 67) because of France's desire to export electricity to Germany. The Germans had then alleged that Électricité de France was subsidising energy-intensive industries and was covering up this by elaborate accounting practises.

The possibility of an internal energy market meant that there was increased political will to deal with such forms of state aid, so it is not surprising that Germany launched its complaints at that time. What is of interest here is that they were not dealt with multilaterally, but *bilaterally* between France and Germany at France's instigation. The agreement between Kohl and Mitterrand in 1989 partially pre-empted the Commission's IEM proposals, or at least attempted to shape the proposals that were to come. France accepted the monopoly status of the German utilities and a modification of the common carriage proposals, as well as the phasing out of coal subsidies at a later date than that demanded by the Commission. In return Germany would to open its borders to imports of French electricity, and the energy companies from the two countries agreed to develop joint ventures. The agreement embraced the aspects of the IEM that were advantageous to both parties.

The Commission did not react negatively to the agreement. In general it still seems to support 'negotiated solutions' between states and sets of states – there have been many such 'subplots' and they are seen as facilitating the integrative work of the EU. Another reason for the Commission's positive view may be that such a major trade-off between the two most important EU actors was the only way to move ahead with the IEM. In other words, unless these actors were satisfied the IEM would not progress.

Padgett (ibid., p. 69) concludes that this is an indication of how powerless the Commission really is. However this ignores the way the Commission works – it is fully aware that it has to have the support of most governments, and therefore it proceeds slowly. The more that can be negotiated between the states themselves, the easier the progress in the Council. Put another way, without the IEM the bilateral agreement between France and Germany might never have been conceived and the issues would not have been on the agenda.

The Commission's role is thus not powerful in the traditional sense of wielding material or economic power, but rather in terms of agenda setting. We will return to this in the final chapter.

Further bilateral energy cooperation resulting from this agreement has developed: Électricité de France' and Preussenelektra AG, and Bayernwerk AG and RWE Énergie have formed two joint ventures – one in the Eastern part of Germany, the other in France – to build power stations, possibly with French nuclear technology (*Energy in Europe*, November 1989). Thus the two governments have been able to agree on mutually beneficial market concepts and market sharing. The political-level agreement has therefore facilitated the work of commercial actors and defined the rules they should follow, while in effect also excluding partners from other countries.

This is a prime example of how the IEM can be used to further domestic energy interests, and it also shows how influential the French government is in forging this type of agreement. France seems to have been able to use the IEM to further its domestic energy interests very well. The promotion of its electricity interests is the major case in point: Électricité de France had been suffering losses at home, and had repeatedly been accused of underpricing its electricity in order to assist and thus attract energy-intensive industries. But with the liberalisation of the electricity markets in Europe a large export potential opened up (ibid., 20 April 1990).

While the government supported electricity liberalisation because it would lead to further exports of French electricity, it has vigorously opposed the proposal for third party access to electricity transmission. It has stuck to its domestic single buyer model with the modifications proposed in the Mandil Report, and has not been willing to change this despite strong pressure from the Commission and the British and German governments in the four-year negotiations over the draft directive. The final agreement in the Council was that the French single buyer model would be made compatible with the Commission's original third party access proposal. This was also an issue of disagreement within the Commission itself: the Competition Directorate maintained that only third party access was compatible with the competition legislation (*EER*, 16 June 1995; *EC Energy Monthly*, 16 June 1995). There was widespread dissatisfaction with this: it was felt that the Commission was being forced to modify its proposal along French lines and eventually to produce a report on the merging of the two systems (*EC Energy Monthly*, 23 February 1995; *EE*, 24 March 1995, appendix). In this case the French government successfully pursued French interests by resisting EU-level changes in the organisation of the electricity sector.

Furthermore France has effectively used environmental issues to argue for the promotion of nuclear energy. As France is at the forefront of both waste treatment and nuclear construction, the government has pointed to the need for new energy facilities in Central Europe and for the replacement or updating of old nuclear plants. The wish to promote nuclear energy also forms the basis of France's stance on the carbon tax. It wishes the tax to be applied to CO_2 emissions only, as this would be beneficial from the nuclear point of view.

In general the French state appears to be making very good use of the opportunities offered by the IEM. Whenever possible it has supported the IEM proposals (*International Gas Report*, 23 June 1989), even when this generated domestic opposition, as in the case of the first directive on third party access to gas. It has promoted its nuclear industry by raising environmental arguments and through its support of third party access to electricity. Former Minister of Industry Roger Faroux has stressed the importance that the French government attaches to the IEM, saying that 'the IEM is vital to our electricity export interests' (*EC Energy Monthly*, 5 September 1989). The benefits of the increased exports of electricity were already evident in 1991, when Électricité de France increased its profits over the 1990 level by $250 million. Although this could be considered far from spectacular, the extra amount was deemed 'honourable' by the president of Électricité de France in view of the fact that it is 'an enterprise that does not have profits as its major goal' (*European Energy Report*, 6 March 1992). However, as we have seen, the part of the IEM process that entails the possible dismantling of national monopolies on gas and electricity have not been received favourably. There is thus a limit to how far the government is willing to go in integrating energy policies.

Britain

The British reaction to the IEM has been positive and Britain has pushed for similar liberalisation measures in the EU as have been enacted domestically. However one argument against the IEM has been that it may entail even more 'Brussels bureaucracy'. Work towards the IEM was predated by the British freeing of the domestic energy market through extensive privatisation. There has thus been no opposition to or major policy interest in the IEM as such, however opposition has been voiced over proposals that could fall under the heading of a common energy policy. Problems are likely to arise in areas such as the environmental impact on the energy sector, the perceived need for the Commission to develop a community sense of security of supply and the move to introduce energy into the EEC treaty.

General antipathy towards any proposal that involves planning and increased bureaucracy in Brussels is a hallmark of the British attitude. For example the IEM proposal to inform EU members about plans for energy investment was opposed because of the fear that this would mean some sort of transferral of power to the Commission, although in fact the draft directive was very innocent in this regard. Britain has maintained a negative stance towards the coordination of any aspect of energy policy in Brussels.

In the areas where domestic legislation has preempted the IEM proposals, however, Britain has been one of the strongest supporters of the IEM proposals, for example those on price transparency and transit directives. In fact the domestic British policy on, for instance, price transparency is far more radical than the EU proposals, and domestic coal subsidies have been reduced to below the EU target (*EC Energy Monthly*, April 1989).

With regard to the directive on public procurement (discussed in Chapter 1), the British fear was not of potentially lost markets but more of increased Brussels bureaucracy. The inclusion of the energy sector in this directive was opposed vehemently (ibid., 7 November 1989). The same fear of new rules and bureaucratic jobs is reflected in Britain's stance on the transit proposals for electricity and gas. Here the British government argued that the rules of competition in the Treaty of Rome provide sufficient basis for free transit enforcement (ibid., 10 June 1989). Similarly, in the process towards third party access in the electricity sector Britain has fought against the French single buyer model, arguing that only the former can ensure open access to electricity transportation.

In summary, Britain has been an ardent supporter of the IEM but only in aspects that concern the application of competition legislation and the creation of a liberalised market. It has opposed any move that might entail a more central role for the EU, especially the Commission. This is in line with the general British attitude towards integration.

Italy

Italy has been an enthusiastic supporter of all IEM legislation, but insists that security-of-supply concerns should override those of the free market. This is hardly surprising in a country that imports 80 per cent of its energy. The government wants improved market effectiveness through the IEM, but not a loss of political power in the market. As such it favours the EU exercising power in the sector, not that the IEM should entail a loss of such power.

The overall impression of Italy's role in the IEM process is that it is 'proceeding cautiously, with plenty of coordination, but nevertheless always endorsing more integration in principle' (*EC Energy Monthly*, 5 September 1989). One senior Italian executive has described Italy's involvement in EU energy policy as 'pretty feeble'. Italy has rarely been at the vanguard of activity.

Together with the SNAM, the national monopoly in gas transportation, the government opposed third party access but accepted the open access and price transparency directives, as well as the public procurement directive, despite ENI's, the major public energy company, opposition to the latter. In general then, as the minister of energy stated, 'the government favours the IEM directives'.

As discussed in Chapter 2, the Italian domestic energy sector is heavily dominated by state-owned enterprises. However they often enjoy independence from the government, a phenomenon known as '*sottogoverno*'. It is very likely that the government favours a strong EU energy policy in order to cope with the sector. There are so many problems in the domestic energy sector that Italy needs a strong energy policy in the EU. The implication of this is not the 'state should be rolled back', as Thatcher put it, but rather that a strong state presence is needed in order to change market rules (ibid., December 1989). There is no clearly defined state strategy towards the IEM, only general approval, nor is there strong domestic interest group opposition to the IEM proposals.

Summing up, the four governments have different records on the IEM. France is clearly the most active participant in the process, and has sought to use the IEM regime in a bilateral agreement with Germany. Germany was unable to make full use of the Commission's pressure to abolish the *Jahrhundertvertrag*, but nonetheless it has benefited from the Franco-German agreement. Britain and Italy have been rather passive participants in the process: Italy seems to be hoping for more intervention on the part of the Commission in restructuring the domestic energy segment, and has few domestic energy interests to promote. Britain sees energy as part of the general transformation that deregulation and possibly privatisation under the general internal market concept would bring about, and strongly favours direct application of competition legislation in this sector.

The other states have largely followed their own energy interests, and while Belgium favours both the IEM and a common energy policy beyond it, the Netherlands has been wary of any change in policy competences in favour of the EU, however informal. It has also opposed the third party access proposal, siding with national energy industry groups. The 'cohesion' countries have not displayed outright enthusiasm for the IEM, but have given their support on condition that EU funding will be provided for the development of infrastructure.

Governments and the common energy policy

We shall now examine the attitudes of the member governments towards the proposed common energy policy (CEP). The cases discussed below are the proposal that the treaty be revised to include a formal competence for a CEP, the carbon tax proposal and the European Energy Charter.

The treaty revision

At the Maastricht summit three governments vehemently opposed the inclusion of a chapter on common energy policy in the Treaty on European Union. Not unexpectedly, these were all energy producers: Britain, the Netherlands and Germany. None of these governments accepted the creation of a formal competence for a common energy policy, and as the proceedings were subject to majority voting the chapter on energy was deleted from the final text. Thus the Commission suffered a setback in its ambitious plans for a CEP (interview, January 1992; *EC Energy Monthly*, December 1991).

As discussed above, the German government is constrained in the issue area of energy whereas Britain has a clear ideological commitment to a freer market through liberalisation. In addition, these states have their own energy resources and do not wish to relinquish their control over them. Both Italy and France favour the inclusion of an energy chapter in the treaty, although for France 'this does not seem to be a particular priority in the final stages of the political union negotiations' (*EC Energy Monthly*, November 1991).

Although the final treaty did not include a chapter on energy, the Commission has not given up hope of creating such a competence. It published a Green Paper on a common energy policy in early 1995 as an input to discussions between member states on the subject and later in the year this was followed by a White Paper on the same topic. France's reaction to the Green Paper was cautious, and eventually it rejected the inclusion of a chapter on energy in the new treaty, Calling was for more 'intergovernmental cooperation', instead of 'new EU tools to manage energy policy' (ibid., 16 June 1995, p. 18). Furthermore France considers that different energy forms should be dealt with at different political levels – only in terms of gas policy for reasons of supply security does France see any role for the EU.

Britain opposed the proposed chapter, arguing that 'the Commission has all the powers it needs' (ibid., 16 May 1995). Furthermore the so-called Westendorp Report, which contained the prenegotiation reflections of member states, found that there was no basis for a formal EU competence in energy policy (*Reflection group report*, para. 141, 5 December 1995).

The energy charter

France showed an interest in the multilateral coordination of energy policy in 1991 when it applied to join the IEA (*Le Monde*, 25 January 1991), but has been much less positive about the energy charter. A major concern is France's fear that non-nuclear countries will delay the protocol on nuclear energy and that non-Europeans will be included in the charter.

Britain, on the other hand, strongly favours the charter because it will extend the liberalisation of the energy market to all of Europe (*EC Energy Monthly*, 15 March 1991), but it does not favour a new EU institution to administer the charter. The IEM element of the charter is thus readily accepted, whereas any elements that could lead to a transferral of power to the EU institutions or a new supranational institution are not. The British essentially see the charter as a free trade regime in energy, where the main task *vis-à-vis* Central Europe is to assist in the transition to a market economy. This is also the view of the German government. The need to establish Western commercial conditions is stressed, and that the major role should be played by private firms. EU administration of the charter should be as minimal as possible and both countries see it as advantageous that the US and Canada join the charter (national non-papers, 1990).

Both Italy and France seem to view the charter as an EU initiative that is intended to form the basis of a general and comprehensive policy towards Central Europe and Russia (national press, 1990). Initially France was not very interested in the charter, fearing that it would slow down work on the IEM. It also resisted the scope of the charter, especially as it extended beyond Europe to include, *inter alia*, the US. Another concern was that the French nuclear interest *vis-à-vis* Central Europe would not receive sufficient attention (Interviews, Oslo, Brussels, 1990). However, as the work progressed France began to participate fully. This indicates that it may have feared being left out and perhaps becoming marginalised in the process.

Italy supported the charter from the beginning and publicly declared itself an 'umbilical cord' between the gas reserves of Algeria and Central Europe. Italy has also already been active in promoting the building of new local gas networks to serve the major lines through Italy into the former Yugoslavia, from where gas can be piped to Hungary, Slovakia and the Czech Republic.

Both Germany and Britain seem only mildly concerned about domestic energy interests in their attitude towards the charter. Britain does not seem to fear competition from Russian gas, or if it does, this is outweighed by the market opportunities that might open up in Eastern Europe for petroleum technology. For Germany the charter will cement its already considerable long-term trade relationship with Russia (Stent, 1981). Here foreign economic and foreign policy interests coincide with energy interests. The stress on the importance of private energy actors in the charter context matches the importance of private actors in the domestic energy sector.

France's reluctance to become involved in the charter process cannot be explained by domestic energy interests. France has a considerable interest in exporting energy technology, especially in the nuclear sector. There is, needless to say, a major growth potential in Central Europe and Russia in this sector. The overall dominance of Germany in the reconstruction of Central Europe and in trade in gas with Russia is indisputable. Germany might therefore be expected to become the dominant state in the charter work. This fear is expressed by French concern about possible delays in the protocol work on nuclear energy. Another French concern is that the US should not be included in the charter – this would eliminate competition from US firms in the region, and would be consistent with France's traditional perception of the limited role the US ought to play in Europe.

Domestic energy interests alone cannot fully explain the various governments' attitude towards the charter process. Fear of competition from Russian gas seems to play very little if any part in the determination of British interests, whereas France's traditional foreign policy orientation seems to explain why it wants to exclude non-EU nations from the charter process, especially the US. However if only EU members are included the position of Germany might become even more dominant, a French concern that is second only to its reluctance to let the US in.

The institutional basis of the charter was uncertain throughout 1990 and the early part of 1991. Various organisational venues were discussed: the IEA, the CSCE and the EU. Germany, the Netherlands and Britain did not necessarily see that the EU should be responsible for the administration of charter, whereas Italy and France argued in favour of EU institutionalisation. However the quick initiative on the part of the Commission to set up negotiations with Russia made it logical to establish a charter secretariat in the Energy Directorate. The issue was not resolved until autumn 1995, when Brussels was chosen as the base of the charter secretariat. The non-EU member states had favoured Paris, where the IEA is located, and the chairman of the charter secretariat had to emphasise that 'the new organisation is an entirely *independent* international organisation' (*Agence Europe*, 27 September 95, emphasis added).

Meanwhile the negotiations for a second charter treaty have started, with the aim of extending free trade principles to the investment phase of energy trade and production. Thus an attempt is being made to extend the IEM both geographically (to non-EU countries) and in scope, as the IEM rules should not only apply to trade in energy, but also to the pre production or 'upstream' phase.

Energy–environmental policy

The third CEP area is that of integrating environmental policy with energy policy.

The main policy proposal in this respect is the carbon tax. The first joint energy–environmental council in December 1991 failed to reach an agreement on the tax. The least developed countries of the EU – Spain, Portugal, Greece and Ireland – were opposed to the tax unless a mechanism for burden-sharing could be adopted whereby these countries would have larger emission quotas than the richer, highly industrialised EU countries (*EC Energy Monthly*, 16 December 1991). Most governments agreed to the tax in principle, with Germany as its most avid proponent – Germany had already adopted more stringent rules domestically: CO_2 emissions are to be reduced by 25 per cent by the year 2005.

Britain deviated from the common EU position CO_2 emissions should be stabilised at the 1990 level by the year 2000 by insisting on the year 2005 for itself. The British prime minister underlined the importance of a multilateral agreement on a carbon tax: 'There would be no point in improving our performance if others just go on as before' (speech, 25 April 1990).

At that stage Britain, the Netherlands and Belgium were somewhere 'between unenthusiastic and downright hostile' (*Petroleum Intelligence Weekly*, 23 September 1991). France supported a carbon tax that would work in favour of increased electricity use, which would benefit the French nuclear industry, and thought that the tax should be imposed throughout the OECD area. Italy argued for a stringent EU emissions policy. When Italy assumed the EU presidency in 1990 it underlined the importance of taking account of the less developed southern region. The Italian stance was to support a tax in principle, but there was disagreement between the various ministries about what form this tax should take (interview, 1992). The same pattern was repeated in the German case. Even France's support was hesitant in view of major opposition from its oil industry (ibid., 23 September 1992).

The preliminary adoption of the tax in May 1992 was made conditional upon the adoption of a similar tax regime in other trade regions, notably the US and Japan. The only major state to oppose this conditional clause was Germany, which strongly favoured unilateral EU action, reflecting German domestic interests in the area (*EC Energy Monthly*, June 1992).

Of the two states that were reluctant to arrive at a decision about a carbon tax only France stood to benefit in domestic energy terms from such a tax. However even France did not argue that the EU should adopt the tax unilaterally, indicating that although domestic energy interests were an important variable in the German case, they carried less weight in France. A concern for international competitiveness appears to be the overriding explanation for the general reluctance on the part of Britain France and Germany to commit themselves to the tax.

The negotiations continued throughout 1994 and 1995. Britain continued to oppose the tax, and it was finally agreed that only the 'willing' would proceed with a voluntary tax: the Netherlands, Denmark, Germany and Italy (*EC Energy Monthly*, 6 June 1995). Britain has continued to block the policy proposal.

Domestic and EU-level governmental strategies

Conclusions

As discussed above, only two governments – France and Britain – approved the major IEM measures during the first stage, while the third party access proposal received support from Britain alone. All the other states opposed it as it would be counter to the preservation of a strong state presence in the energy sector (*EC Energy Monthly*, April 1992).

Britain supported all proposals that explicitly aimed at the liberalisation of energy markets, notably the opening up of transmission grids, but opposed investment transparency because it might entail increased bureaucracy in Brussels. It could be that Britain was pursuing a political strategy aimed at creating IEM rules that would benefit British domestic energy interests. However evidence points against this, for two reasons: (1) the British government has divested itself of most policy instruments in the energy sector: (2) it has no national energy policy. Hence there is no basis upon which to assess which EU-level would allow Britain to optimise its domestic energy interests. The third party access rules of both stages one and two (the 1989 and 1991 directives) are less radical than domestic British legislation, and the British energy industry is subject to a more stringent regime than its competitors on the Continent. It would thus seem advantageous for Britain to attempt to shape the IEM rules in accordance with its own regime. However the British attitude has been to *respond* to rather than to attempt to shape *policy* at the EU level.

France, on the other hand, has shown evidence of strategic policy-making at both the domestic and the EU level. Domestically, the government has privatised some parts of the public sector, including energy, and also imposed commercial criteria of action on publicly owned energy companies. The government has retained a major presence in the sector and is able to overrule its own energy companies. A salient example here is Gaz de France's opposition to gas transit liberalisation, which nonetheless was espoused by the government. The domestic strategy of France has been to make its energy sector more market responsive, and also to promote its comparative advantages at the IEM level: here all transit directives have been supported and the nuclear energy capacity has been expanded domestically to meet the increasing export potential for electricity. Furthermore the French government has pursued a strategy of exporting more electricity through its bilateral political agreement with Germany. The role of the French state has been an active one, and it has been able to utilise the function of the state as 'gatekeeper'.

Germany and Italy, however, show no evidence of consistent strategies at either level. Italy subscribes to the IEM proposals, but is seemingly unable to implement them successfully in terms of restructuring the domestic sector. Germany votes with the major interest groups in the gas industry on the transit issue, and as such deviates from its generally favourable position on the IEM proposals. It is unable to utilise fully the opportunity represented by the Commission's demand for coal sector restructuring: it only reluctantly complies with these demands because the opposition from the coal sector is so strong.

In sum, the most influential government in the IEM process is France. Both Britain and Italy have approved the IEM, but their role has been responsive rather than proactive. Germany has the least positive attitude towards the IEM, despite its general emphasis on free market rules.

In the case of the common energy policy, however, a less clear picture emerges. Here Germany and Britain are united in their opposition to the treaty amendments, while Italy and France support them. This attitude corresponds to each government's general view of integration in the EU. The charter has been received favourably by all four states, but again Britain and Germany agree in their advocacy of free market rules, in their aversion to the creation of a supranational organisation to manage the charter, and in their emphasis on the need for a framework agreement to guarantee that commercial criteria will reign in East–West European trade. Italy and France tie the charter closely to the EU process in general, while France wants to exclude non-EU countries.

There is little indication that domestic energy interests influence the states' attitude towards the charter. General EU orientation and the potential to expand foreign trade in the region loom large. France is attempting to promote its nuclear technology by expressing concern over the role of the nuclear protocol, while Germany and Britain merely stress the need for a major role for private companies.

In their attitude towards the carbon tax even less of an energy strategy can be discerned. All four states approve of the idea of such a tax, yet none wish to commit themselves until a global regime exists. In the discussion over whether the tax should be on carbon emissions or general energy use, France is actively promoting a carbon tax. This corresponds to the domestic interest in nuclear energy.

Thus the importance of domestic energy interests for government policy at the EU level differs between the IEM and the CEP. In the IEM process the EU-level positions and domestic energy interests correspond. France is proactive at both levels in pursuing a policy of market liberalisation while protecting domestic energy interests. Britain is consistently defensive at both levels. Italy and Germany have no discernable strategies. With regard to the CEP, the states' attitudes do not reflect energy policy interests but rather a mixture of their general stance on integration and export interests in Russia and Central Europe.

The role of interest groups

Interest groups are important to the general EU policy-making process in more than the traditional way of national lobbying because they are permanently represented on many of the committees through which all draft proposals pass, and are invited to provide input and reactions in the early stages of policy formulation in the EU. The interest groups that are consulted by the Commission in the area of energy include major associations and companies. So far consumer and environmental groups have not been a prominent presence in these discussions. Large consumer groups, especially in industry, have actively lobbied for an internal energy market, but smaller, private consumer groups have been less visible as Brussels lobbyists.

Interest groups play a large role in the energy field. Major energy companies have joined forces to create European federations, and these are well represented in Brussels. Each type of energy has a European federation: oil (Europia), gas (Eurogas), nuclear (Foratom), coal (CEPCEO) and electricity (Eurelectric). These groups play an important role in the framing of policy proposals. They are often consulted by those in the Commission who are responsible for drafting the initial texts, as these federations can provide considerable technical information, and for this reason their input is often indispensable. Their importance also lies in the fact that they are powerful market actors.

Little specific information is available on how the energy groups lobby, but we know from general studies of EU lobbying that interest groups are important in the initial phase of policy-making as well as in more or less permanent working groups and committee. Also, the more technical interest groups lobby the Commission while the more general ones turn to the European Parliament. The latter are typically groups that deal with the environment, consumer affairs and so on (Andersen, 1996). Studies of various policy sectors show that there has been an increase in lobbying efforts in Brussels in the post-85 period. According to Greenwood *et al.* (1992, p. 3) 'the evidence suggests that there is an increasing confidence and familiarity with the European level, and that the "Brussels" route is increasingly being taken'.

As stated above, the major interest groups in the energy sector have formed their own pan-European organisations with secretariats in Brussels (*EC Energy Monthly*, April 1992). They work directly with the Commission as well as with their own governments. Pan-European groups such as Eurelectric, Unice, Eurogas and so on have been specifically set up to influence the EU policy-making process. For the smaller groups with fewer resources it may be easier to seek influence through national representatives, and all interest groups in the energy field have in fact concentrated on national decision-makers. However an increasing number of interest groups are also lobbying the EU directly. The empirical literature confirms that these two arenas are complementary rather than mutually exclusive.

The pan-European organisations have large expert secretariats at their disposal, and are very sophisticated participants in the policy-making process. They publish papers on controversial issues, and these are studied by all the parties involved and duly noted by the press. These groups are represented by speakers at important EU conferences, where at the least the views of the employer and employee organisations UNICE and ETUC are usually represented.

Despite frequent and detailed input into the policy-making process, the impact of interest groups in the IEM process has not been as strong as might have been expected. Substantial effort has been put into changing the IEM, but energy interest groups have not been successful in changing the *general direction* of IEM policy, only in *modifying* particular proposals as well as slowing the pace of dereg- ulation. This has probably come as something of surprise to the interest groups themselves. The explanation for this may lie in the importance of the internal market proper as a general model: much resistance from commercial actors was to be expected but could not be accommodated should the internal market become a reality.

The determination and political leadership of the Commission has been extremely significant in this regard. Whenever interest groups have threatened to stall progress on a controversial issue the Energy Directorate seems to have taken one accommodative step backwards yet two forwards. For instance the public procurement directive was delayed, then amended to become an acceptable compromise, and finally adopted. The same is true of the gas transit directive, where the third party access proposal was modified, yet the second stage of the IEM – represented by the new third party access proposal from the Commission – contained all the industry could ever fear from such a proposal. The pattern seems to be that first the Commission makes a very daring bid – putting into the draft proposal not what it thinks will result but what it ideally would like to see result. Then the long-drawn-out process of negotiation begins, and when the proposal finally results in a directive that is adopted by the Council it has been toned down considerably. Yet it represents another brick in the energy policy edifice.

Interest groups' opposition to the IEM was uniform and persistent in the first and second stages, and particularly intense in the second stage. Coalitions of different interest groups have formed to oppose third party access, and the electricity industry and the public enterprise organisation CEEP have published a paper on an alter- native EU energy policy (*Europe*, 20 July 1992). The Commission's response has been to attempt to coopt the major interest groups into a working group on third party access, with a mandate to work through the third party access concept in detail. Some interest groups have attacked the Commission for attempting to boost its own powers by establishing 'more regulation and bureaucracy', as claimed by the German gas companies (*International Gas Report*, 3 April 1992).

From 1992 the major debate on the IEM centred on third party access to electricity and gas, and with it the role of public service companies. The political process towards third party access stalled at the end of 1995, when it was decided to study the French single buyer proposal in tandem with third party access, thus potentially opening the door for the maintenance of energy monopolies, justified on the public service function as in the SB system. Throughout this period the pan-European energy and industry associations were active in the debate, both as part of the EU system and independent of it.

The most significant change of position was recorded when Eurelectric went from opposing third party access to accepting it, after the consultant firm McKinsey wrote a report on the Dutch electricity sector and recommended that it be opened up to full competition. Ironically, McKinsey had been hired by the Dutch electricity industry in order to investigate how it could best protect its interests in view of the discussions about national deregulation and third party access at the European level. The conclusion was that the Dutch should adopt a deregulatory system akin to the liberalised system in Norway and Britain, and that this would result in financial savings for both the industry and the customers (*ECE*, 21 October 1994). This report led to the Dutch electricity industry changing its view on third party access, and this in turn induced a change in the official stance of Eurelectric, which now called for swift action on the part of all member states to ensure that the market rules for the industry were made uniform; in other words a 'level playing field' should be achieved.

Various deregulatory measures are being introduced in various countries, and this must be harmonised so that international electricity industry knows which rules obtain. From the point of view of any international energy company, it is a major disadvantage to have to deal with differently evolving regulatory environments. Hence the insistence that only EU-level deregulation is appropriate. This shift of strategy and lobbying arena, away from the national level is also strengthening the role of the Commission as regulator.

With regard to the carbon tax and other environmental measures, interest groups are increasingly demanding that all rules must be harmonised so as to avoid distortions of competition. This is evident in the industry's rejection of the carbon tax while insisting that if accepted it must be a tax covering all relevant competitors; in other words it should be a global tax. These interest groups probably had a major impact on the final decision to modify the tax proposal: in the words of a UNICE spokesman; 'The measures to be taken must be universal. The adoption of an energy tax in the EC alone will affect the competitiveness of the EC.' Opposition to the tax proposal by UNICE and the oil industry group Europia has been steadfast and uncompromising: the tax would distort competition, endanger relations with OPEC and other oil producers, and is unnecessary. UNICE has proposed alternatives to the tax that range from joint implementation mechanisms with Central Europe for the reduction of CO_2 emissions to advocating voluntary measures in the industry. In the run-up to the Essen summit in December 1994, UNICE, Europia and many other European industrial associations published a statement of opposition to the tax, mainly because it would distort competitiveness, and advocating voluntary measures instead. A key argument was that energy prices in Europe were already higher than in the US, the EU's main trading partner and competitor (*EC Energy Monthly*, 16 December 1994). Again the argument was for a 'level playing field'.

Interest group opposition to the energy–CO_2 tax has thus been persistent and intense. UNICE has been very active, and the major petroleum groups have followed suit, along with industrial groups such as CEFIC (the chemical industry association), the cement industry and other energy-intensive industries (ibid., June 1995, p. 5, 6/95:5). However, since two of the three countries that joined the EU in January 1995 – Sweden and Finland – already have national carbon taxes, there will be added pressure on the EU to develop a common policy. These countries will support a common stance because of the need for equal competitiveness. There are thus national pressures from below as well as international pressures from above for such a tax. Nonetheless one must conclude that the initial attempt on the part of the Commission to develop a common policy in this area has failed. In late 1995 the Commission started to look at existing policies for energy saving and efficiency measures so that they could be upgraded to fulfil the EU's international climatic commitments (ibid., p. 6).

However the industrial world is split on other key issues. While one branch may agree with the need for common or harmonised rules, and thus favours a strong role for the EU as regulator, another may oppose a common energy policy or third party access under the IEM.

Logically enough third party access is supported by industries that consume a large amount of energy as it will lead to competition in the transmission of energy and thus lower prices, while energy companies, both producers and transmitters, in the main oppose third party access. The European chemical industry association (CEFIC) is pushing for third party access (ibid., February 1994), and the CBI (the Confederation of British Industry) also strongly favours third party access over the single buyer proposal. Likewise UNICE points out that all exclusive rights in the energy sector act to distort prices (ibid.) However, CEDEC, the European confederation of public sector energy distribution companies, opposes third party access, arguing that it would not guarantee supply to all customers and would undermine its members' role as energy monopoly companies. CEDEC was formed in 1992 as a direct response to the IEM proposals on third party access.

The proposal for a formal common energy policy competence has galvanised interest groups, but no major activity was recorded until the topic was reissued for discussion by the Commission in 1994–95. The attitude towards the creation of such a competence is largely negative.

The Energy Charter had the unilateral support of the industry, as could be expected. However Esso France was strongly critical of a perceived policy to strengthen the EU institutions: the charter has been called 'the tree that hides the forest', and it is thought that the development of a secretariat, a base protocol and separate protocols for energy types will necessitate 'the establishment of a heavy, permanent structure of administration and control' (*International Gas Report*, 3 April 1992).

The Green Paper on the CEP received a major input from energy and industry groups during 1994. The paper was not released until early 1995, but in July 1994 the Commission published a preparatory document, asking for written interest group responses. A number of important pan-European groups took this opportunity to influence the very first stage of CEP formulation. The CEEP, the public energy providers' association, argued that security of supply should remain the responsibility of the member states and that it form the cornerstone of energy policy. Energy policy should be policy, not deregulation, and competition in this field would be detrimental to security of supply (*EC Energy Monthly*, 16 December 1994). Eurogas was the harshest critic of many parts of the document, especially those dealing with third party access (ibid., 21 October 1994) – its comments were described by a source in the Commission as 'unhelpful' (ibid., 23 November 1994). However other energy groups did not voice their opposition to third party access on this occasion, but used the opportunity to discuss the form a CEP should take.

There were some differences of opinion among the interest groups representing the various energy forms, Europia, the oil industry group and its 'upstream' colleagues in the E&P Forum stressed that a CEP should be based on maximum reliance on market principles. The EU should primarily focus on providing a stable regulatory environment so as to ensure a level playing field. There would be no problem with import dependence because the market would take care of the matter. Rather the EU should build good relations with oil and gas producers, bearing in mind the importance of OPEC in this regard. The proposal for a carbon tax would greatly complicate the good relationship with OPEC, Europia pointed out, which also saw no need for emergency oil stocks beyond what measures already existed under the International Energy Agency arrangements. The best way of securing gas imports was to continue the present system of long-term supply contracts. As for the environment, there should be no 'excessive or ill-conceived' legislation, and there should always be a cost-benefit analysis when contemplating environmental legislation. In sum, the petroleum industry saw no need for a CEP and certainly not for an IEM – things were alright as they were, and the market mechanism would deal with both the environment and security-of-supply issues.

Eurelectric, the pan-European electricity organisation, wanted a common regulatory framework in the EU, but one that would respect the existing differences in the regulatory frameworks of the member states. This may sound contradictory, but it is necessary to bear in mind that this organisation represents various state electricity industries. According to Eurelectric the EU should attempt to impose common rules of the market, but not to change the structure of the various national sectors. It was feared that the logical consequence of third party access would be a strong controlling force in Brussels: 'Central planning at the EU level would be unwieldy, would increase the scope for political interference in business decisions and would be contrary to the idea of increased competition' (ibid.) On the environment, Eurelectric concurred with the oil industry and defined the EU's role as one of harmonising environmental rules across the states – the level playing field argument again. The EU's role should be to represent EU interests in international negotiations and promote voluntary approaches within the industry. In sum Eurelectric saw no need for a formal CEP competence to be enshrined in the treaty.

The interests of the coal sector are promoted by CEPCEO, the association of European coal producers. It argued the need for a security of supply policy, pointing out that coal is both indigenous and plentiful in the EU. It favoured a strong EU role in creating such a policy, which should aim at diversifying fuel sources. This, incidentally, would promote coal. On the environment, CEPCEO argued that there was great need to get around this problem by employing clean coal technologies.

Finally, the UNICE and IFIEC, representing employers and general industry, concentrated almost exclusively on promoting competitiveness. Energy markets should be open and competitive, and as for the environment, it would be best served by a good investment climate, which would enable companies to afford to modernise their equipment and employ environmentally friendly technology.

The nuclear industry has been largely without a lobby group, but Foratom, the European federation of nuclear trade associations, has tried to increase its role since about 1995. Several import policy decisions must be taken on the future role of this energy type in the EU, as the entire nuclear sector in Eastern Europe remains a major headache for the EU. While Foratom aims to create good trade relations for the upgrading of nuclear power stations in Eastern Europe, it recognises that the future may be fraught with problems of liability in the case of accidents. It looks to the EU as the actor most able to solve this problem through bilateral or multilateral agreements.

In conclusion, interest groups in the energy sector have pursued their strategies in both the national arena and at the EU level. There has been extensive activity at the EU level by the most important pan-European associations such as the UNICE and ETUC, as well as by the groups that represent the various energy forms. Both the electricity and oil lobby, together with UNICE, favour common EU rules in order to level the playing field, and thus have chosen to forego national policy advantages. Other energy associations disagree, especially gas and coal.

There was a shift in the venue of lobbying activity in the period 1985–95, and although national lobbying continues, the EU has become an increasingly important arena.

Conclusions

The various EU governments' attitudes towards the IEM have been largely consistent with their national interests, but their stance on the various CEP proposals reflect a more complex picture.

In Germany the government has promoted its coal interest, but has also argued that it is bound to adapt to EU rules in this area. A precarious balance has been maintained between supporting the national coal sector and criticising it. Britain's support for the EU proposals has been firm, but there again national legislation had preempted much of the IEM. However it has shown little enthusiasm for the CEP proposals because of its fear that the Commission will use the CEP to enhance its own role. France has displayed the most consistency and has been able to use EU-level policy to its own advantage, promoting the IEM only when it has suited its national energy interests. France has insisted on retaining the energy companies in public hands and there is still a strong government presence in the energy sector. Finally, Italy has responded positively to almost all the IEM measures, perhaps because it does not have well-developed energy interests of its own to defend.

The four states' approach to the CEP proposals have not followed energy interests *per se*, but rather more broadly defined interests in foreign trade policy and policy towards Eastern Europe, especially with regard to the Energy Charter. On the carbon tax, those states that already have a tax favour an EU-level tax.

Interest groups have been active at both the national and the EU level, but their activity at the EU level has increased. The large pan-European energy associations have provided input into EU affairs and there is evidence that they have come to favour a common deregulatory framework for energy policy in the EU so as to achieve a level playing field.

6

The Role of EU Actors

The EU institutions and decision-making after the SEA and TEU

This chapter analyses the part played by institutional EU actors in the IEM and the CEP processes. The overall objective of this and the next chapter is to assess the importance of the role these institutions play in comparison with that played by the member states, as discussed in the previous chapter. We are concerned here with the *relative* importance of the various institutions *within* the EU. The assessment of the relative roles of member states *versus* EU institutions is presented in Chapter 7.

There is hardly a 'standard' or 'typical' EU policy-making process since many types of actor interact with one another via many channels (Nugent, 1994). The procedures used depend on the type of policy area in question and the type of legislation sought. Most legislation is administrative and regulatory, involving the application of EU law to particular cases. This is undertaken by the relevant directorate and does not surface in any political debate or conflict. However when an issue is of prime political interest, or is controversial, it usually requires the full legislative process. This means that a draft directive is presented by the Commission for further decision-making. This is the case with all internal market legislation.

Although not originally intended, unanimity became the rule for Council decision-making after the French demand for this in Luxembourg in 1966. The Single European Act (SEA) changed this in requiring that all internal market legislation be reached by qualified majority voting, called the cooperation procedure. The treaty revisions at Maastricht added a third procedure, the codetermination procedure, whereby the European Parliament was endowed with more power.

The cooperation procedure demands two readings in the Parliament instead of the one that prevails in the consultation procedure, where the Council reaches a decision either by qualified majority vote or unanimity. In the cooperation procedure the Council can only adopt a common position after the initial reading in the Parliament. If there is disagreement over Commission amendments, which are usually effected after the Parliament's opinion has been heard, the Council must act unanimously. In most cases a common position is reached in the Council, and this is communicated to the EP for a second reading. Within three months the Parliament must accept the common position, reject it, amend it by an absolute majority of all members, or do nothing. If the Parliament accepts the common position, at second reading the Council makes it into legislation. If the Parliament has rejected it, the Council can only adopt it unanimously. If the Council does not accept the Parliament's amendments, again it must act unanimously.

The implications of this new procedure is that the Commission, the Parliament, and the Council work much more closely together since they depend on each others' cooperation in order to have a proposal adopted. It is difficult to reach unanimity on a controversial proposal, and it is difficult to mobilise two thirds of Parliamentary votes in order to reject or amend. Finally, it is vital that Commission proposals allow room for compromise and negotiation.

Thus a *new incentive for cooperation* between the three formal decision-making bodies of the EU has arisen since the Single European Act. Furthermore, the time limit imposed by the cooperation procedure has speeded up the decision-making process considerably, and links between the institutions have improved. There is general agreement in the literature that these procedural changes have acted to intensify EU-level activity. However one should not assume that an oppositional situation existed previously between the institutions – since Commission officials have had to deal time and again with the same representatives of the member states, a conflictual model of Commission–Council relations is misleading (Ludlow, 1991). Proposals have been 'chiselled out' *en route*; and the results of many influences are incorporated into draft directives before the informal reading in the Parliament and the final decision-making in the Council.

The general decision-making process in the EU always seeks compromise and unanimity where there is conflict. However until the SEA there was little incentive to find a common stance since there was no threat of being outvoted. Now there is such an incentive, and this has acted as a disciplinary force on the cooperation between the EU institutions and on the various national interests involved.

The above discussion deals with the formal apparatus of the EU and the formal rules that pertain to it. However scholars have increasingly come to describe the EU as a 'network' (Bressand and Nicolaides, 1990). Keohane and Hoffmann (1990) describe the EU as a network that 'involves the pooling and sharing of sovereignty rather than the transfer of sovereignty to a higher level', where in the policy-making process 'the formal and informal institutions at different levels in the formal structure, if in the formal structure at all, are linked by a variety of networks'. The incentive for decision-makers is thus to cooperate in creating 'packages' and 'linkages' where different interests may be accommodated. Interest groups of various kinds are found both within the formal structures as participants in consultative committees, and partly outside it yet in consultation with the Commission. The opportunity for creating useful linkages is therefore good. Linkages occur between sectors and are typically concluded at a high political level, such as in the European Council. Wessels (1990) describes the 'package deals' that result from these meetings as the major instruments of progress within the EU.

This chapter investigates the part the various EU actors have played in the preparatory work for IEM and the CEP. The relevant actors are the Commission (the Energy, Environment and Competition Directorates), the European Parliament, the European Court of Justice, the Council of Energy Ministers and the European Council.

The Commission

The actors within the Commission

The Commission functions as the initiator of all policy, guardian of the treaties and the implementing body of much policy. It is also the drafter of texts, another very crucial role (H. Wallace, 1990). In terms of the energy sector, the Commission's exclusive right to initiate policy is a most important one, as is its capacity to intervene in its role as guardian, although this role is much more limited for practical reasons.

The most substantial part of policy-making is the drafting stage, which is the work of the Commission alone. The 'products' that result are legion – expert reports, policy papers, studies, programmes and formal policy proposals in the form of draft directives, based on draft communications. This agenda setting may be important not only for defining policy problems and their subsequent solution, but also for defining member states' positions at the later stage of negotiations. Learning and persuasion are two key words here – participants in the agenda-setting stage have the advantage of framing the policy to be suggested to decision-makers. We should therefore pay attention of interest or position formation: do actors come to EU negotiations with domestically defined national interests, or are their positions influenced by how the Commission frames the policies?

The main actors in energy policy in the Commission are DGXVII (Energy), DGIV (Competition), DGXXI (Customs Union and Indirect Taxation), DGXII (Research and Technology) and DGXI (Environment). Proposals that come from one directorate have to be 'cleared' by the others, so internal differences between directorates have to be resolved before a proposal can be sent on to the Parliament.

A draft directive in the making is discussed by various committees and interest groups, and the latter are often standing members of such committees. The policy proposal eventually presented to the Council is thus familiar to the various national and other actors affected. On their way to the Council all proposals are examined in great detail by COREPER (Comité de Représentants Permanents), which has almost 200 subcommittees at its disposal. National representatives thus influence policy documents at various stages. The decision-making system represents a mingling of purely national interests with those of the EU as a whole.

In comparison with the many committees and their experts, the number of people employed in each directorate is small, and consequently they are bound to need the advice and comments of many external experts on particular aspects of proposed policies. Yet even though a small directorate may nonetheless be able to define a policy interest for itself.

Within the Commission the Energy Directorate is naturally the major actor in energy policy, and it considered by many to be very responsive to energy industry interests (interview, Brussels, 1990), which is not surprising in light of the close cooperation between it and the interest groups in the area. An Energy Directorate representative even expressed the view that if the EU were unable to implement IEM proposals due to interest group opposition, the European Council might intervene. This indicates that a certain apathy may be felt by the directorate's staff at times, and also that the possibility of intervention from above is ever present. The European Council can thus impose a Community interest when the particular and sectoral interests become too identified with interest groups in the sector itself.

The Competition Directorate (DGIV), has a more confrontational role *vis-à-vis* business groups as it intervenes directly when EU competition rules are violated. As will be discussed in the next subsection, throughout 1990 and 1991 this directorate assumed a much more active role in this respect than ever before, including in the energy sector. The Competition Directorate has the power to intervene in all instances of unfair competition based on the Treaty of Rome rules governing the 'abuse of dominant position' (para. 86 EEC).

The mere existence of a monopoly is not enough to prompt intervention; there has to be a situation of 'abuse'. This previously meant that a complaint had to be brought to the directorate, or that the latter intervened only after a situation of conflict had arisen, with the result that the directorate had no occasion to intervene in the monopoly structures in the energy market. However after 1990 a more active role was assumed whereby the competition commissioner began to intervene directly in monopoly structures in the energy sector, demanding that member governments should either justify the maintenance of monopoly companies or abolish them (interview, Brussels, 1993). Ludlow (1991) pointed to the growing assertiveness of the Competition Directorate in the latter part of the 1980s, and found that it was due to a more favourable attitude among the member states towards EU intervention. Formal rules are thus utilised by EU actors depending on their reading of the political legitimacy of an action at a given time.

Energy and environmental policy have been integrated since June 1990 and the Energy and Environment Directorates now cooperate closely. Environmental policy proposals are presented by the Environment Directorate, as was and also the proposal for a carbon tax, which is both an energy and an environmental issue. Council meetings are attended jointly by the energy and environment ministers when cross-disciplinary issues are on the agenda; otherwise the usual, separate councils are held. All matters involving indirect taxation –

for example the carbon tax proposal – are also discussed with the Customs Union and Indirect Taxation Directorate, which is responsible for fiscal matters.

However in energy policy it is the Energy Directorate that proposes the major part of all legislation. The former commissioner for energy, Antonio Cardoso e Cunha, was a very active proponent of the IEM and of an enhanced role for the EU in the energy sector, and he repeatedly gave voice to the strong ambitions of his directorate. A typical example is the way in which he seized the opportunity presented by the Gulf War to propose a supranational role for the EU in emergency-oil-stock measures and in the IEA (*Europe*, 30 August 1990). Cardoso e Cunha also travelled to energy-supplying countries, for example to Algeria to discuss EU–Algerian cooperation in the building of new pipelines, thus developing an extensive 'energy diplomacy' network (ibid., 26 May 1990). The Commission is able to decide whether financial aid should be provided to such projects because transportation facilities are essential to the success of the IEM. The Commission has therefore assumed responsibility for the development of the European gas grid. It was given a formal competence for this in the Treaty on European Union, *after the Energy Directorate had developed such a policy role for itself.*

Not only the energy commissioner but also the former president of the Commission himself, Jacques Delors, took an active interest in energy policy. Delors' interest seemed to lie in the integrative possibilities inherent in energy trade. He was a vital influence in the Energy Charter process, which was introduced at a European Council meeting by a member state and then 'taken over' by the Energy Directorate and promoted by Delors on several occasions as the best way of bringing about interdependence and integration between East and West. He referred to the charter in his speech to the CSCE at the signing of the Treaty of Paris in November 1991, and also mentioned it in other speeches. While the energy policy implications of the charter were important to Delors, clearly the 'high politics' consequences and possibilities remained vital.

Much of the possibility for political strength of the Commission lies in this diversity: the basics of a policy area are dealt with by the relevant directorate, yet at the higher level, package deals and linkages are created such that compromises are made possible and enlargement of the scope of the issue area is ensured. At the summit meetings in the European Council, the president of the Commission can forge such linkages between and within policy areas.

The Energy Charter is an example of this kind of multilayered policy-making. First, it is an extension of the IEM, thus satisfying the ambition and tasks of the Energy Directorate; second, it involves East–West European cooperation, and thus links energy policy with EU policy concerns towards Russia and Central Europe; finally, as all the industrialised nations are signatories, the EU has been placed at the centre of policy-making in yet another sector.

The versatility of the work that takes place in the Commission is a key to understanding its central role in the EU. It has instruments and agents that can legitimately deal with many facets of a policy area, but this versatility can also be a drawback in the sense that policy can become more disjointed than coordinated. For energy, the policy possibilities include the environmental dimension, the East–West European dimension, the internal market dimension and the competition dimension. There is a corresponding variety of actors under the Commission's aegis to deal with all these facets – the directorates, the committees, the head of the Commission, and so on. Thus the Commission is well equipped to draw up a policy agenda and its exclusive prerogative in this respect must be considered important.

However energy policy still lacks a proper legal basis. Nugent (1994, p. 229) cites economic and monetary policy, industrial policy, energy policy and regional policy as four policy areas that do not yet possess 'strong and integrated policy frameworks'. The IEM does have a solid legal basis in the 1985 White Paper as well as in the Treaty on Political Union amendments – the chapter on networks is really about creating the IEM – but nowhere is there a legal basis for developing the CEP.

The Energy Directorate's role in the IEM

We turn now to the role of the Energy Directorate in the IEM process. The first stage of the IEM, consisting *inter alia* of the transmission directives for gas and electricity, was presented in 1989. Both the 1988 report on obstacles to the IEM and these draft directives proposed a modified form of third party access. This met considerable opposition among member states as well as from the energy industry. When the package was discussed by the Council of Energy Ministers in May 1990, the draft directive on gas was returned to the Commission for lack of agreement. However, the electricity transit directive was adopted at that meeting. The Energy

Directorate modified the gas transit directive so that only energy transmitters would be allowed third party access, and listed the 29 eligible transmitters in Europe. Even with this modification, Germany voted against the directive when it came on the Energy Council agenda in October the same year.

Two insights about the work of this directorate are important here. First, compromise was sought in the prolonged process of modification that took place after the Council failed to reach a viable agreement the first time the directive was on the agenda. Second, after a certain degree of modification the directive was returned to the Council, where it was adopted despite opposition. The directorate had staged many informal and formal meetings with interest groups in the search for compromise, and the second version of the directive represented the furthest it could go in modifying the proposal while retaining the IEM concept as its guide.

In 1990 the Energy Directorate then proceeded to the second stage of the IEM. It set up four working groups consisting of national representatives, interest groups and Commission officials in order to work on the further opening up of the electricity and gas markets. Opposition to the IEM, especially from industry, was thus *incorporated* into the process in a much more formal way than hitherto. These working groups spent a year and a half on the task, and published their reports on recommendations for further work before the Commission presented its communication on the same subject.

The second stage of the IEM restated the original aim of allowing consumers third party access. However these would have to be consumers of large amounts, thus excluding individual households. This represented a compromise over the original common carriage proposal in the 1988 document on the internal energy market. Again much opposition ensued from industry and member states. Like the first directive on gas transit; the contents of this draft directive were ambitious, and thus it was highly unlikely to be accepted in its initial form. As we have seen, the negotiations over this directive continued for several years. In autumn 1995, there was general agreement on a modified version with regard to electricity, but gas had not been dealt with at all by that time. The major opposition from industry was partially expunged by long-term cooperation in the working groups and the consequent maturation of the Commission's ideas.

In 1992 the Commission established an expert committee on electricity transit whose task is twofold: advising the Commission when it so requires, and proposing conciliation measures in the case of conflict between market actors over transit. The committee consists of representatives of the grids, independent experts, one representative of Eurelectric and one of the Commission. Although the outcome of any conciliation is not binding, it can be assumed that conciliation has an important role to play. Moreover this is an example of how the Commission brings together the main actors in a contentious policy area in an attempt to bring about develop a common view. As part of a formal committee the protagonists are required to cooperate over a long period of time; in this case four years.

Theoretically, the Treaty of Rome contains the necessary legislation to enable the Commission to demand immediate open access (paragraph 90). However in stage two of the IEM the Commission instead chose the cooperation procedure based on paragraph 100A. This is because a consensual, albeit slower, decision-making process seems to be sought whenever possible in order to achieve as much legitimacy as possible for a given policy. However the possibility of resorting to paragraph 90 remains. As we shall see in the next section, the Competition Directorate in particular has insisted on using this paragraph. The Competition commissioner has consistently argued that the IEM should be constructed with the use of competition legislation, a view that has been supported by Britain because it would ensure the creation of common market rules for energy rather than a common energy policy. But the energy commissioner has also used the threat of competition legislation to put pressure on the member governments in the stalemate over electricity transit.

All coal investments must be approved by the Commission, as laid down in the ECSC treaty. In the summer of 1992 the Commission prepared a new decision on coal subsidisation to be presented to the Council for unanimous acceptance, as required by the ECSC rules. This replaced a 1986 directive (2064/86/ECSC), and was designated to create more competitive conditions in the coal industry. Member states that continue to provide state aid must now submit biannual plans for this to the Commission for its approval, and aid cannot exceed a certain level relative to a market price for coal determined by the Commission. Aid to the coal sector is now part of the general EU state aid policy and the sector no longer enjoys a privileged position. The IEM principles have thus been strengthened in the sense that all sectors requiring aid will receive it as a transitory arrangement on the road towards greater market responsiveness at some point in the future. The important difference between earlier EU coal policy and the new direction lies in the fact that maintaining a certain level of coal production is no longer sufficient to warrant state aid. Instead it must aim at rendering the plant in question more competitive or at creating alternative employment. This amounts to 'a significant tightening-up of Community policy' (*EER*, June 1992; *Europe*, 25 July 1992), which again was arrived at without any *change in formal competence.*

The Commission has thus brought coal policy into line with the common market philosophy and the IEM principles in restating the original aims of the ECSC treaty. There was never any intention of letting each state decide how much aid should be provided to its own coal sector, however this has been the reality in most of the EU's history. The change towards a more common coal policy is thought to have been made possible by the increased acceptance on the part of the states for the general internal market project. The IEM and the general increase in legitimacy for its realisation has thus made it possible for the Commission to tighten up the provision of state aid. A consequence of this is that the Commission has strengthened its role *vis-à-vis* the governments by forging an EU-level aid policy for coal.

The restructuring of other energy aid programmes must be seen in this context. By creating a common umbrella for evaluating and granting aid, the Commission has acquired informal CEP-type powers through the logic of the IEM. In other words, informal integration in energy policy has taken place.

The Energy Directorate's role in the CEP

The Commission has also been extremely important in initiating the CEP. Here there has been no guiding concept, although in a general way the internal market rules stipulate what must be done in the energy field in order to conform to a set of core principles. There is no explicit mandate and no common vision of what a CEP should entail, or indeed why it should be created in the first place. The CEP is almost wholly the brainchild of the Commission, and it has tried to create it by using the IEM as its mandate and guiding logic, and by defining CEP proposals in ways that highlight the advantages to member states of an EU-level policy. In this endeavour it has been only partially successful.

External events have presented important opportunities in this regard. Without precipitative events in the form of the changes in Central Europe and the former Soviet Union, as well as the Gulf

War, the major CEP policy proposals would hardly have materialised.

The proposal to include energy in the TEU treaty revisions came from the Energy Directorate and was part of its general proposal for treaty revision. The rapid extension of the EU energy agenda in the wake of the external events made it important that energy policy in the EU should be provided with a legal basis. It was also in the interest of the Commission to seek a formal competence in this area as it would consolidate its energy policy role. The treaty revisions are really only a *formalisation* of the process of energy policy-making initiated by the Commission.

It is important to emphasise that the IEM remains a vital part of EU energy policy, but that it is necessary to go beyond this for in several reasons: with regard to the environment, security of supply and the role of the EU as an international actor. The energy commissioner suggested a security of supply policy for the EU, to be brought about in stages over several years, with the clear aim of pooling member states' energy reserves. The suggestion for an emergency oil mechanism was part of this general policy, but was presented as a consequence of the Gulf War. At the same time the commissioner mooted the idea that the EU should apply for membership of the International Energy Agency and appear as a unilateral actor in that forum.

Apart from a few member states, such as Belgium and Italy, few actors other than the Energy Directorate have voiced a need for a legally based CEP. However, both the security-of-supply policy and the merging of environmental and energy policy may necessitate such a basis. Elements of energy policy clearly fall under the legislation on competition policy; for instance, the lack of gas transit possibilities is arguably an abuse of monopoly position. Legally the Commission could base all its policies relating to the creation of a freer market in energy on this legislation. However the existence of a legal basis may not be enough, or it may not be necessary. Common policies could be based on Article 235.

The competition rules have been in place since 1957, yet have rarely been used in many sectors of EU policy simply because there has been a lack of political will among the member countries to 'activate' the rules. The internal market concept represents a restatement of the competition rules, and as such provides a political mandate for them to be used actively. Paradoxically a CEP may materialise *without a legal basis* in the treaties if there is sufficient political will behind an individual proposal. Some members, for example Britain, have argued that as the transit proposals for gas and electricity fall under the competition rules, the Commission should simply base its decision-making on paragraph 90 and not bother with the fully-fledged political process of paragraph 100A.

However the Commission will certainly strengthen its potential to develop a CEP if it acquires a legal basis for the development of a common energy policy. It is precisely in periods of widespread opposition to such a policy that a legally based competence for it is needed. However such a competence could only be established if the member governments were to push for greater integration. A logical strategy for the Commission, therefore, would be to try to establish formal acceptance of such a competence when the degree of government support for the IEM process is at its strongest. It is thus logical that the Commission should be preoccupied with the CEP at the time when the states are concerned with the IEM, and that it should utilise the general governmental support for the IEM to try to forge a CEP.

This makes for an interesting observation with important implications for integration theory: in periods of intense governmental activity at the EU level, such as during the post-1985 period, governments are able to reinforce their power. The Commission and other EU institutions can do the same; but they need a large degree of acceptance from the states for their general work, and only when this exists can they seek to strengthen their powers in a given policy area. In other words, *in periods when there is little integration neither the states nor the EU actors can increase their influence in policy-making, whereas in periods such as the post-1985 one, both sets of actors do.* EU policy-making need not be a zero-sum game, as intergovernmentalists assume, but may in many cases be a sum-sum game because two sets of actors look for different outcomes. If the Commission is able to design a policy that both satisfies the states and strengthens its own role it could be successful in its pursuit of a CEP.

In the case of the treaty revision, however, what in effect would be a unilateral transfer of power from the states to the Commission was too much for most states to accept. However policies can come about in a variety of ways, and the outcome of the treaty revision was an EU-level competence in the area of infrastructure, something that is also an important part of a CEP. Furthermore, as the agenda-building in the energy issue area extends, the discrepancy between the lack of a legal basis and the policy content increases. The perceived need for a legal basis for a CEP is then more apparent, and this may increase the willingness on the part of the governments to consider establishing such a basis.

When the proposal to add an energy chapter to the Treaty on European Union was turned down, the Energy Directorate turned its attention to preparing for the intergovernmental conference in 1996 and the treaty revisions on the agenda there. Its argument was that 'energy is a strategic good rather than a commodity, and needs its own legal base rather than being tackled via the Treaty's environmental and market rules, or the catch-all Art. 235' (*EC Energy Monthly*, 16 May 1995). By stressing the non-market aspects of energy policy, for example geopolitical factors, the Commission was building its argument that there should be a CEP as well as an IEM. Its work towards the new treaty revisions was marked by careful overtures to the member states – in its Green Paper (EU, 1995) it tried to show that the latter needed and would benefit from a CEP.

Turning now to the European Energy Charter, there were several possible fora for the political process. Nevertheless the Energy Directorate came to play the leading role in this process too.

When the idea of the charter was raised by the Dutch premier Ruud Lubbers in June 1990 the European Council responded favourably, and during the course of autumn 1990 several of the member states began to formulate their views on the subject. Neither the Netherlands, Germany nor Britain were particularly keen on the EU being chosen as the charter organisation.

In October 1990 the Energy Directorate held talks with Russia on the subject of the charter. At that time the EU member states had made little progress, for instance France not only lacked information on the charter process but also failed to take much interest in it (interview, 1990), while Germany and Britain were preoccupied with where the seat of the charter should be. Meanwhile the Energy Directorate continued its negotiations with the Russians, and was therefore the natural institution to develop the preliminary text of the charter, which was presented in the early part of 1991. The first charter conference took place in July the same year, the second in the autumn, and the charter was eventually signed in December 1991, just a year and a half after the idea was proposed by Ruud Lubbers. At that time there was no longer any discussion about what role the EU should play *vis-à-vis* other international fora in this process (*Europe*, 13 April 1991; *Petroleum Intelligence Weekly*, 2 December 1991), the EU had become the leading policy-maker in the process and proceeded to set up a section in the Energy Directorate to work exclusively on the charter.

In this case the Commission had initially been given only a very general mandate by the European Council, but while the states were trying to decide which international organisation should be the seat of the charter, the Commission had gone to work and had completely taken over the process by defining the topics for negotiation, and then, after this framework had been established, presenting it to the states. The charter is an excellent example of the overriding importance of the *initiating* role of the Commission in policy-making. The states were almost presented with a *fait accompli*.

The second charter conference started in 1995, and the Commission were successfully argued that Brussels was the best location for the charter secretariat, now a permanent international organisation, because of the 'synenergy' possibilities. It was also able to promote the charter idea as the institutional basis of the Euro-Mediterranean conference that started in autumn of 1995. Thus the Commission had developed a new institutional device for dealing with third countries, based on the IEM concept. The declaration from the first conference on this reads: 'we acknowledge the pivotal role of the energy sector in the economic Euro-Mediterranean partnership [and] decide to create the appropriate framework conditions for investments and the activities of energy companies' (Barcelona declaration, 27 November 1995). The energy aspects of the partnership between the EU and the Mediterranean countries will be linked explicitly to industrial cooperation through the ministerial conferences to follow. The charter has thus proved a useful tool for the Commission.

We now move on to the proposal for a carbon tax. This proposal started with the decision taken at the European Council meeting in Luxembourg in 1990 to stabilise CO_2 emissions at the 1990 level by the year 2000. At the previous European Council meeting in Dublin in June 1990 it had been decided that energy and environmental policy should be coordinated. The next step was a communication from the Commission 'A Strategy to Limit Carbon dioxide Emissions by the year 2000', that formally proposed a carbon tax. The first joint energy–environmental council meeting to have this on the agenda was held in December 1991, and Commission was asked to study a number of questions before the Council could decide on a specific tax.

The Environment and Energy Directorate's were given joint responsibility for the carbon tax process. However in early 1992 disagreement between the two commissioners became apparent.

Energy Commissioner Cardoso e Cunha echoed the concern of interest groups and member states that a carbon tax must not be a unilateral EU move, while the Environment Commissioner Ripa de Meana wanted the EU to take the lead in the international community prior to the UNCED conference in June 1992. This conflict was reminiscent of the familiar intraministerial rivalry of domestic politics. Within the Commission proposals that involve more than one directorate are cleared with the others concerned. In this case the proposal was a joint one, and agreement had already been reached on the need for the tax – the area of contention was the role of the EU *vis-à-vis* other trade regions: the US and Japan. The final adoption of the tax was made conditional upon the adoption of a similar tax burden in other trading blocs, and as this failed to materialise, the tax was vetoed by Britain in subsequent council meetings.

The two directorates had to withdraw their original tax proposal (COM/92/226) and issue a modified version in May 1995. This time the tax was made optional, as the member states had insisted. However this applies for a transitional period up to the year 2000 only, after which there should be a uniform EU-wide tax, according to the Commission. Needless to say this version of the tax proposal has also elicited strong negative reactions from both member states and interest groups.

The role of the Commission in the carbon tax process was threefold: first, at the European Council in June 1990 it proposed the merging of energy and environmental policy; next it put the emission stabilisation proposal on the agenda of the European Council; and finally it commissioned a report on the usefulness of fiscal measures as a basis for its own proposal for such a tax.

At the same time, the legal basis of environmental policy in the EU was being generally strengthened in the run-up to the TEU revisions. An obvious strategy was that integration in the treaty of a legally 'strong' environmental policy with the 'weak' energy policy area, as stipulated by the treaty, would indirectly strengthen the status of energy policy and thus contribute to a CEP. The attitude of the member states in this policy process was at best reluctant. None were eager to see a carbon tax accepted, apart from Germany, which had adopted more stringent domestic emission-reduction policies than those set by the EU. For the Environmental Directorate, the adoption of such a tax would give a major boost to its importance within the hierarchy of directorates. It would be the first case of an EU tax, and of the integration of an environmental policy – in the form of a tax –

into the internal market rules. Also, adoption of the tax before the UNCED conference in June 1992 would make the EU a notable international actor in this policy area. This was very important to the environment commissioner, who repeatedly challenged his colleagues in the Commission on this, threatening not to participate in the UNCED conference unless he could bring a dowry, as he phrased it.

As matters turned out, the EU neither played a key role at UNCED nor at the first conference of those party to the climate convention in Berlin in 1995. It had proved impossible to forge a common EU climate policy because of the controversial tax proposal.

The European Court of Justice and the Competition Directorate

Since the Competition Directorate (DGIV) applies competition legislation and the European Court of Justice (ECJ) pronounces judgements on the correct interpretation and application of the legislation, these two bodies are dealt with together in this section.

The ECJ has supranational powers in some areas of legal competence, among them competition policy. Its rulings supersede national law and directly affect the member states. The ECJ has gradually but steadily enhanced its role as an EU actor, and member states have by and large accepted the self-proclaimed supremacy of its rulings, and have not caused problems over the fundamental issue of who is *der Herr der Verträge*: who it is that makes the ultimate decisions – the national courts or the ECJ. The ECJ, like the Commission, has been very active since 1985.

The IEM is based upon the competition policy of the Treaty of Rome, but also on Article 100A of the Single European Act, the so-called 'internal market paragraph'. This is the domain of Competition, the most powerful directorate in the Commission. It is authorised to raid, without prior notice, the premises of any company suspected of violating competition rules, and can also fine such companies. Complaints about its rulings are heard in the Court of First Instance (Jacobs and Stewart-Clark, 1991).

It is noteworthy that the legal apparatus for dealing with obstacles to competition has existed since the signing of the Treaty of Rome, but that it has only been applied extensively to the energy sector since 1990. This naturally has a lot to do with the political will to tackle the energy monopolies. In interviews in the Competition Directorate we found that willingness to tackle the energy sector began gradually to increase from 1990 onwards.

In general the Competition Directorate has intensified its work towards greater competition in the energy sector as part of the internal market process. In April 1991 the commissioner announced that two sectors vital to the internal market needed attention – telecommunications and energy (*Europe*, 6 April 1991) – and he sharpened the definition of permissible monopolies: 'They can only be allowed if they are absolutely necessary for the provision of a public good which the market is unable to provide' (ibid.) In effect this means that gas and electricity monopolies must be dismantled, both in terms of import and export monopolies as well as monopolistic pipelines. The Commission asked all member states that have such monopolies to abolish them or justify their necessity. According to the directorate, they are unlawful under Article 37 of the EEC Treaty (ibid., 22 March 1991). This was the first step of a legal procedure to force the member states to dismantle the monopolies. In the telecommunications sector the ECJ upheld an intervention by the Competition Directorate to abolish special rights for some national telecommunications companies.

For energy, the aim is to arrive at free competition while ensuring security of supply and uninterrupted supply, according to Sir Leon Brittan, then commissioner for competition. In his statement on competition policy in the directorate's annual report in 1990, Brittan stressed that a major aim was to achieve competition in sectors previously characterised by state monopoly, and that only minimal norms would apply in sectors where a public service function such as gas, electricity, the postal service, transport, banks and broadcasting could be said to exist (*Europe*, 24 June 1991). In addition to the reduction of state aid to the sector the aim is an intensification of the practise of fines, administered by the Competition Directorate.

The Commission has consistently invoked the internal market mandate in sectors where competition legislation has been lacking or never applied. It has done this strategically, starting with the 'easiest' sectors such as telecommunications and transport and then moving on to notoriously difficult, heavily monopolised sectors such as energy. The Commission's interventionism has been supported by the rulings of the ECJ, but the Commission first tries political methods, via directives, to achieve its goals. When this has proved impossible it has turned to direct intervention, using its legal powers, which naturally is highly controversial. In the stalled negotiations over third party access to electricity it consistently threatened court proceedings, but in the end it instead accepted a compromise solution.

Sandholz's (1992) major study of EU telecommunications policy in the post-1985 period showed that the Commission played the leading role in creating an internal telecommunications market as part of the general internal market, and that in 1988 the Commission had taken a tough deregulatory approach against the interests of the states by basing a controversial directive on paragraph 90 EEC, which does not require Council approval. This directive, which is aimed at creating an open market in computer terminals and services, stated that monopolies in the sector were abusing their dominant position. Commissioners feared that, by invoking paragraph 100a, the directive would be delayed and watered down considerably in the Council negotiations. The interesting issue here is that all the member states agreed with the policy objective of the directive, but they strongly disagreed about the use of paragraph 90, which would 'set a precedent for Community activism', as some put it. Nonetheless the Competition Directorate proceeded to issue the directive. France immediately filed a suit with the ECJ to challenge the Commission's use of paragraph 90. Although Germany, Italy and Belgium supported the French case, the ECJ ruled in favour of the Commission. Without the strong general support of the member states to create an internal market in telecommunications the Commission would hardly have dared to invoke paragraph 90. Thus a precedent was set for the Commission to make use of competition policy. But the political cost of doing this may be considerable, and will probably be higher in the case of energy than in telecommunications.

Since 1985 the Commission has also clearly intensified its application of competition legislation to the electricity sector. McGowan has studied the Commission's role in the deregulation of the electricity market and concluded that:

It was only in the mid-1980s that the Commission demonstrated both the willingness and the competence to challenge the national utilities which had previously been effectively protected from Community purview by member states. The new developments occurred in the context of . . . the internal energy market. The Commission launched this initiative on the back of the revival of its authority following the SEA . . . and the Commission's increased readiness to apply competition law. This increased activism of antitrust affected public enterprises and public utilities in particular. In cases concerning the telecommunications and transport industries, the Commission effectively established precedents for action in the energy industry. (McGowan, 1993, p. 44)

There was thus an intelligent use of 'spillover' here: since the Energy Directorate has no formal competence in EU-wide energy policy, it used competition legislation in areas where it could obviously be applied – for example transportation and telecommunications – in order to set a precedent for defining energy policy, especially in terms of gas and electricity.

The ECJ has also helped with the creation of the IEM. In a ruling in Spring 1994 (*Almelo* v. *Ijsselmij*, C393/92) the ECJ ruled that electricity is like any other good and is not a public service. This was a landmark ruling because it means that competition rules can be applied to the energy sector just like any other sector, despite the claims of the industry that trade in certain energy types, for example gas, are characterised by 'natural monopolies'. This was the first ruling to state that the provision of energy is not primarily a public service. In this ruling public service was defined in a rather narrow way, using paragraph 90,2 of the EEC. Companies must now demonstrate that they need *restrictions* in market rules in order to perform a public service function if these restrictions are to be allowed.

This ruling may be very important for the Commission in an ongoing court battle: in June 1994 it took five national energy monopolists to the ECJ over monopoly import and export rights in gas and electricity, having tried unsuccessfully to deal with this issue through bilateral negotiations with the states concerned. Because of the Almelo ruling the Commission can count on a favourable interpretation of monopoly and public service practises, although the ECJ has yet to rule on the interpretation of the public service function and what it entails. While the Almelo ruling determined that electricity (and by implication other forms of energy) is a good and not a service, there is still no authoritative interpretation of what a public service function means in terms of monopoly companies. The question of whether the energy companies' monopoly over imports and exports is justifiable because they are obliged to render a public service remains unanswered. In June 1994 infringement proceedings started against five member states – Spain, the Netherlands, France, Ireland and Italy – because of their import and export monopolies.

There is, as recounted above, some political movement on third party access, but with the outcome of the above mentioned court case pending the Commission has sought to resolve the issue by bringing a series of other cases before the ECJ. According to one commentator: 'Undoubtedly, the Commission had hoped that its draft legislation . . . would have made faster progress . . . and that such confrontationist tactics would not be necessary' (*EC Energy Monthly*, September 1994, p. 4). In the present case the Commission is arguing that the public service function does not justify the existence of import and/or export monopolies. Nor is security of supply an adequate reason. If the ECJ agrees with the Commission, this could very well mean that the question of transmission will also be brought before the court: it makes little sense to uphold exclusive transmission rights unless exclusive import and export rights are also retained. The Commission thus hopes to be able to institute the IEM through the application of the competition legislation in court proceedings. This is the only route available when the negotiated approach fails, and it allows pressure to be brought to bear during political negotiations.

Through these examples we can see that the IEM is intimately connected with competition legislation and the general internal market mandate. The Commission has met so much resistance to its proposed changes to the energy sector that it has been forced to argue in terms of competition legislation and the general need for an open market: the existence of import and export monopolies is hindering progress on third party access, and vice versa.

In 1993 the court ruled on six important energy cases out of a total of 1250 running cases on restrictive practises and possible abuse of monopoly position. Only about 10 per cent of all cases were initiated by the Commission. In its report for 1993 (COM94/161) the Competition Directorate stated that the IEM is still a key priority, 'despite the difficulties of introducing the dynamics of competition into a sector that has long been shielded from competition and the application of the treaty rules'.

In sum the Energy Directorate is trying to bring about the IEM through negotiations at several levels, whereas the Competition Directorate is following the logic of bringing the energy sector into line with deregulation in other sectors. In this the latter has been greatly aided by the ECJ. Since 1990 the Competition Directorate has boldly applied competition legislation to telecommunications, transport and finally energy, using precedents established for the former sectors as bridgeheads to reach the energy sector.

The European Parliament

The European Parliament is playing an increasingly important role in the energy sector, and may in fact be the Commission's foremost ally in energy policy. Since the signing of the Single European Act and the Treaty on European Union it has played a greater role than before, and it has a considerable interest in the environmental side of energy policy. EP members are grouped in interparty alliances, or political groups.

The EP's main work in any given sector takes place in specialised parliamentary standing committees. There are 18 of these, each with 30–50 members. The EP's Committee for Energy, Research and Technology (CERT) is concerned with consumer affairs and environmental issues to a greater extent than what seems to be the case with the Commission (interview, Brussels, 1990). Former energy Commissioner Cardoso e Cunha stated that the political long-term views on energy policy ought to come from CERT, while the 'nitty-gritty' of energy policy should result from work with the Council. CERT is sceptical about the virtues of market liberalisation, and has protected what it sees as the interests of consumers and the environment. CERT has 28 members, the socialists being the largest group with nine members, closely followed by the Conservatives. The Environment Committee, which also deals with relevant energy cases such as the CO_2 tax, has 44 members and here too the socialists are the largest group. CERT arranges hearings with interest groups in an issue area and then forms its own views on the basis of this input. These hearings involve various independent experts, interest groups and so forth. The energy and environmental commissioners attend hearings regularly, and take part in the discussions (*EC Energy Monthly*, November 1990).

On the 'energy package' discussed earlier (stage one of the IEM), the EP agreed to the general lines of this but suggested the EU might aim at a more comprehensive energy policy than that implied by the IEM. This, it was pointed out, would be necessary in order to take account of environmental factors (ibid., October 1989). There was agreement that the EP must defend consumer and environmental interests, and stimulate the political will to achieve this. Third party access and increased gas use are key elements of a policy towards this end, and environmental criteria for energy policy are being promoted. The EP wants more political power to achieve environmental and safety goals (*Europe*, 7 April 1990), and CERT has placed special emphasis on consumption patterns in the transport sector and has a positive view on a carbon tax.

In addition CERT has called for a 'greener' energy charter that stresses energy efficiency and is more critical of the role of nuclear energy in Eastern Europe. MEPs have called for the Commission to prepare a 'strategic plan for nuclear energy in Eastern and Central Europe' (*EC Energy Monthly*, 11 April 1994). The EP has consistently been critical of nuclear energy and of the possibility that the latter may be presented as environmentally sound.

CERT has made very strong pronouncements against the principle of subsidiarity being applied to environmental policy, as laid out in the Treaty on European Union. This would, in its opinion, mean a less forceful policy in this area because the necessary degree of supranationality would not be ensured. This is an argument for increasing the role of EU institutions in general and the role of the EP in particular in this policy area (*EuropeEnvironment*, 30 June 1992).

The EP thus appears to be representing the interests of the environment and the consumer. Andersen and Eliassen (1990, p. 316) find that, 'in emerging and politically highly potent sectors as the environment . . . the new procedures between Parliament and Council seem to have strengthened the role of Parliament'. Lobby groups appear to find it increasingly necessary to talk to members of the EP, and the rapid mobilisation of public opinion in many European nations on issues related to the environment makes the EP an important forum in which to highlight such issues. Judging from the amendments made on energy proposals, the EP favours the development of a common energy policy, and will probably make the environment a cornerstone of its proposals on the latter. Indeed between 1985 and 1995 the EP consistently stressed the need for a CEP, arguing that energy policy goes well beyond market concerns and that the EU should coordinate a common policy. It must be added that this would also boost the influence of the EP.

Once a parliamentary committee has issued a report outlining possible amendments and its overall conclusions, formal voting takes place in the plenary EP. However little time is allotted to discussion prior to voting, and the language problems make spontaneous discussion difficult. Often the voting takes place at a different time from the discussion. It thus seems that the *impact that the EP has on legislation primarily takes place in the appropriate committee.* The hearings arranged by CERT have been very well attended by interest groups and also by Commission officials, and key committee members are in close contact with Energy Directorate officials. The names of a few politicians in the energy–environment area crop up time and again in connection with policy discussions, and these key politicians have good contacts with environmental lobby groups in Brussels (Interview, Brussels, 1990). There is thus an identifiable and small network of people in the EP and the Energy Directorate that interact between themselves and with key interest groups.

Thus, the *formal* role of the EP is not its only importance; the *network* of persons that the various policy sectors in the EP draw on is perhaps more important. Since parliamentarians are generalists, only a few of them with special interests and abilities are able to deal with Commission experts on an equal basis. It is these few that define the EP's response to Community policy in their area, and through their contacts with NGOs, the press, and national groups at home they may exert a considerable influence in controversial matters. It is therefore important for the Commission to enlist the support of the EP, and indeed the networks in both institutions do cooperate. Ludlow's (1991) point that the EU institutions are partners, not adversaries, is relevant. The cooperation procedure is built on this realisation and seeks to strengthen it by providing incentives for further institutional cooperation between the EP and the Commission. The codetermination procedure described earlier strengthens the interdependence between EU institutions further and allots a more important role to the EP. It should also be noted that the amendments made by the EP after the adoption of the Single European Act codecision procedure have been largely accepted.

Overall the EP appears strongly critical of the IEM as an energy policy regime but favours the establishment of a CEP. A CEP would serve to strengthen the EP's insitutional basis *vis-à-vis* other EU institutions as it would imply an enhanced policy-making role for the EU in general. This could in turn allow the EP to advance consumer and environmental interests in energy policy. Antonio La Pergola, a former member of CERT, expressed the need for a CEP that would take care of regional development of the energy sector as well as preserving the 'public functions' of energy companies. Stating that market forces can not solve the main problems in the energy sector, he called for an interventionist policy on the part of the Commission. Such a policy, in his view, already has a legal basis in paragraph 90.2 of the Treaty of Rome, which recognises that some economic services should be public ones, and that arguably this also applies to the energy supply. Furthermore, a CEP would serve the interests of the consumer, with whom the EP is concerned. La Pergola's view is typical of the views expressed by other MEPs (interview, 1992).

Claude Desama, former president of CERT, specified the conditions required for CERT to support stage 2 of the IEM proposals. These centred on the need for accompanying policies to deal with environmental concerns and security-of-supply problems. If third party access does go ahead, CERT is critical of its implications for individual consumers who are unlikely to be in a position to negotiate over sources of supply. Third party access is therefore likely to benefit large industrial consumers only. In addition it has been questioned whether the IEM will be compatible with environmentally friendly energy policy (*Europe*, 17 April 1992). The role that the EP will play in stage 2 of the IEM is considered by Desama to be important since the Commission will need allies: and the EP may utilise this when bargaining with the Commission over amendments to draft directives. The EP's call for a CEP was voiced further in a resolution expressing regret that the chapter on energy had not been included in the Maastricht treaty (*EC Energy Monthly*, April 1992) and in its support for such a chapter to be included in the treaty revision at the intergovernmental conference in 1996. It has also called for a chapter to be included in the Euratom and ECSC treaties. Furthermore the EP has called for strong energy policies *vis-à-vis* Central Europe and the Mediterranean, as well as for a carbon tax and for greater attention to be paid to the environmental aspects of energy policy (ibid., October 1995).

However the formal role of the EP in the energy policy-making process must be considered fairly insignificant. It favours more of a CEP-type policy than the IEM proposals, but there is little evidence that it has had an impact on the direction of policy development, in spite of its support of the Commission and its sometimes radical policy proposals. Nor have the interests of consumers and the environment, as espoused by the EP, figured prominently in the process so far.

The Council of Energy Ministers

Governments meet in the Council of Ministers to adopt or reject directives. Their voting strength varies according to size of country, but not proportionally so. The actual taking of a vote happens relatively rarely in the Council, but the second reading of the gas transit directive in October 1990 was an important exception. Here a vote was taken since Germany in particular could not reach a common position with the other countries.

As a rule the specialised councils, including energy, meet twice a year, and consist of the national energy ministers, their civil servants, the energy commissioner, Commission officials and members of the cabinet of the commissioner. Usually more than 100 persons attend a given Council meeting, which typically lasts for two days. The Council presidency, which rotates every six months between member states, is important in eliciting compromises. The presiding country is responsible for seeking out such compromises, often by contacting each delegation separately. Most countries wish to achieve a good 'output' during their presidency, and thus have an incentive to succeed with whatever work is currently on the EU agenda. The relevant commissioner is similarly engaged in negotiating and he or she can change draft proposals throughout the negotiations in order to reach a compromise.

National interests are what is at stake, and before the Single European Act there was no real incentive to reach agreement because of the unanimous decision procedure. However the threat of casting a vote on a controversial matter has induced a willingness to compromise that is markedly stronger than before. This was illustrated by the decision-making on the IEM directives: Germany was opposed to the open access directive for gas, so instead of forcing a vote – and a defeat for Germany – the Council postponed the decision until the next session. In the meantime the directive was reworked in order to find possible common ground. However this endeavour failed and there was no alternative but to hold a vote on the directive at the next Council in October 1990, where Germany was the most prominent of those voting against it.

In the first council discussion on stage 2 of the IEM much opposition to third party access was voiced. This was an informal meeting, intended to reveal the extent of the disagreement: 'While the tenor of this gathering swung from outright hostility to apparent attempts to build bridges, the end results appeared to be fairly severe entrenchment on both sides' (*International Gas Report*, April 1992). In the following four years there was progress on various parts of the IEM, but not on the essential third party access proposal. As discussed above, it has never been accepted by all member states, and the decision at Essen in late 1994 was to study it further, along with the French 'single buyer' proposal. In their opposition to third party access the key member states have been siding with the oil and gas industry. Even if a general agreement was found with regard to electricity in autumn 1995 – a merging of the SB and the third party access models – so much real disagreement remained that the Council meeting in December 1995 had to be postponed. The Commission reacted strongly to this and repeated its threat to invoke Article 90. According to the Commission, 'completion of the single market is an obligation arising from the Treaty of Rome' (*Europe*, 13 December 1995).

Thus negotiations continue in and between Council meetings, where they may very well end in postponement if there is something to gain from this. The Commission is involved in the negotiation process, from the inception of the draft document until every possibility of compromise has been exhausted in the Council. The conclusions from the Council proceedings are notably rather vague about who had opposed what, thus protecting the deliberations from public scrutiny. This may well be an important explanation of why negotiations can continue for so long in Council meetings (Wessels, 1990), although the threat of arriving at a decision by the majority voting procedure has in fact led to a greatly enhanced policy-making capacity on the part of the Council and decisions take much less time than before (H. Wallace, 1990) – few if any member states wish to stand out as a reluctant participant in the internal market endeavour.

The European Council

The European Council plays a major role in providing the Commission with a general mandate for policy-making. At the biannual summits the heads of the member states often make a general linkage between policy areas, indeed this has become a central task of the Council. In the case of the IEM the European Council mandated the Commission to pursue matters relating to the internal market in general. In the case of the CEP, both the charter and the merging of environmental and energy policy were explicit acts of the Council.

Only the treaty revisions originated from the Energy Directorate itself.

The role of the European Council has become very central since its formal inclusion in the Single European Act. Although it has no formal role in the internal policy-making structure of the EU, its importance clearly began to increase in the latter part of the 1980s. The more integrated the EU institutions become, the more pronounced the need for member states to legitimate this.

The Council of Ministers officially enters the decision-making process only during the *final* stage, whereas the direction of EU policy is indicated from the *beginning* by the European Council – 'indicated' because the mandate given to the Commission is always cast in very general terms. Thus it may be said that the Commission enjoys wide powers of policy definition and formulation despite the increasingly important role of the European Council.

At the European Council meeting in June 1992 in Lisbon it was stated that the energy charter work 'will facilitate the transition of East-Central Europe towards a market economy and enhance environmental protection'. However, the negotiations on the Basic Agreement had been in a stalemate for some time, so the Council intervened to try to rectify this: the European Council emphasizes the importance of the rapid progress in the negotiation of the Basic Agreement and urges the charter conference to intensify its efforts in order to reach early agreement (Presidency Conclusions, 1992).

The European Council thus monitors the progress of the EU agenda, points to expected developments and may urge the speeding up of the policy process.

Conclusions

The record on the IEM hardly indicates a march towards success, but rather a gradual process whereby Community viewpoints seem to have won ground through modification and interest group mediation. The Commission has postponed controversial proposals and has worked closely with the energy industry, but in the end it has been able to ensure the adoption of those directives that are most important to the logic of the internal market. The foremost example here is the gas transit directive, which for a long time was opposed by the major gas producing and transmitting countries: the Netherlands and Germany. Since it proved impossible to reach a unanimous position on this controversial issue through painstaking negotiations, the Commission finally resorted to majority voting – and won. This illustrates the new strengths of the EU institutions: if the usual method of consultation and negotiation does not work, the Commission may resort to alternative procedures.

Furthermore, it seems clear that the Commission is playing a much more active role in breaking stalemates than it did prior to 1985. A statement by an Energy Directorate employee to the effect that 'higher powers' (meaning the president of the Commission) would intervene if the IEM stalled, testifies to this. The very logic of the internal market demands that no sector should lag too far behind in implementing the basic principles of the four freedoms: transport, persons, goods and capital.

This conclusion may seem obvious, but it is important to recall that almost the entire energy industry, especially the gas sector, was united in its judgement that open access to gas transportation would not be adopted. The fact that major interest group opposition has not hindered the adoption of controversial proposals shows that the logic of the internal market is stronger than sector interests, despite the fact that the Energy Directorate is alleged to be very responsive to wishes of the energy industry. Phrased differently, the general support for the internal market concept emanating from the states is stronger than the issue-specific opposition of interest groups and a few of the member governments.

The role of the Council of Ministers is essentially one of *adoption* or *sanction*. The major part of policy-making in the form of negotiation or bargaining takes place in the many committees and during informal consultations. The *process* itself is therefore central to the determination of the contents of policy. Consensus is always sought, and reaching a consensus is also important to the participants. This makes access to and participation in the decision-making process *prior* to the final deliberations of the Council of Ministers vital.

The Commission is the initiator of this process, and is also the 'broker' of interests. The national representatives play the *dual* role of defending national interests and pursuing a consensus, as W. Wallace (1990, p. 235) points out. The need for common interests to be defined is imposed on member states in their capacity as members of the European Council. Thus the forum for voicing purely national interests remains the Council of Ministers, but by that stage much of the policy-making has already been done.

The sanctioning ability of the Council is indisputable, but this is a rather negative capacity in a decision-making system that aims at consensus. Here the ability to forge linkages is very important. In this both the European Council and the Commission play a vital part.

With regard to energy, however, the role of the European Council is relatively unimportant and is confined to the provision of very general guidelines. It is the Commission that proposes the contents of policy. The European Parliament has never used its powers of amendment in the energy context; it has merely expressed opinions on the general character of the proposals, although these have been critical enough. Both the Competition Directorate and the European Court of Justice have played a key part in applying competition legislation to the energy sector, and the former has been especially active since about 1990.

7

EU–Member States' Relations: Empirical Conclusions and Theoretical Implications

Member governments and the energy policy-making process

In this chapter we shall attempt to assess the relative importance of the various EU actors in the energy policy-making process. This may be an attempt to 'square the circle', as it were; that is, the outcome of such an exercise depends very much on whether it is possible to quantify influence in the same way when we evaluate the role of the various actors. We have assumed throughout that member governments' energy interests are largely fixed prior to the start of the decision-making process at the EU level, and that they use the EU as an arena for furthering these interests, both at the EU level and domestically, in line with Putnam's model, described earlier. In Chapter 2 we discussed the nature of these government interests.

However when we discussed the role of EU actors and institutions we could not employ this framework of analysis. Essentially neorealist in origin, Putnam's model assumes away the influence of these actors in conceptualising the EU simply as an arena. But in the empirical analysis of the roles played by the Commission and the European Court of Justice we found that they wield a direct influence not only by applying competition legislation but also by setting the agenda. In the case of the Energy Charter, the Commission can be said to have designed the policy in its entirety, whereas the member governments only developed their positions during the course of the negotiations over the treaty. Thus Putnam's approach is not useful when analysing the role of EU actors. Below we shall first recapitulate the empirical findings and then move on to a discussion of how to evaluate the role of EU actors and non-state actors such as interest groups.

Chapter 2 concluded with an assessment of the capacity of each of the major states to control domestic energy policy. Italy was found to have a pervasive presence in the energy sector, yet was constrained in its ability to implement policies. Another constrained actor is Germany because of the heterogeneity of the energy actors in the federal system and the largely privatised nature of the energy sector.

The two other main governments – France and Britain – are determined to be autonomous actors although they differ greatly in their involvement in the sector. While France has upheld state ownership of the major energy companies, Britain has privatised them. However the British state has withdrawn as a result of a political strategy, not because interest groups in the sector forced it to do so. The relative influence of both states in the sector is therefore large – or at least potentially so in the British case – despite the choice of different strategies domestically.

Chapter 5 analysed the part played by of these states in EU energy policy-making. A classification of the strategies of the four states in domestic-level policy-making and in the IEM is illustrated in Table 7.1.

France

Of the four states in this study France has been the most active in the IEM process. It has sought to shape the IEM in a way that benefits its domestic electricity interests, and has thus pursued an offensive

TABLE 7.1

States' domestic and IEM strategies

	Domestic level	IEM level
France	Has adapted somewhat	Is shaping the IEM
Germany	Has adapted somewhat	Mixed response
Italy	Has not adapted much	Accepts the IEM
Britain	Has adapted already	Is shaping the IEM

international strategy. In addition the French government has reached a bilateral agreement with Germany that furthers its domestic energy interests. Finally, France has been able to adjust domestically to the IEM regime as the latter has evolved: it has sought to impose commercial criteria on publicly owned energy companies and has carried out a certain amount of privatisation. It has, however, chosen to retain ownership of the energy companies in order to maintain its political influence over the sector, as discussed in Chapter 2. This domestic strategy is being pursued in opposition to stage 2 of the IEM proposals, especially as regards third party access.

Germany

Germany has no clear domestic energy strategy. When the Commission intervened in German coal policy, ruling that the *Jahrhundertvertrag* was against the competition rules, there was no protest from the German government. However the trade unions and the coal companies took the Commission to the European Court of Justice. When the plaintiffs requested the support of their government it was not provided, but only suggested as a conditional option should all negotiations with the Commission fail. This indicates that the government was to some extent constrained by interest groups – it had to give them some public support.

If it had been able to, the German government would very probably have used the EU demands as a weapon against the domestic coal companies and trade unions, thus adopting an offensive international strategy to solve a domestic problem. However the German government was not autonomous enough to do this. As we know, it was the *Bundesverfassungsgericht* that ruled on the legality of the *Kohlenpfennig*, thus there are several actors in Germany that impact directly on the energy field.

Italy

The presence of the Italian government is pervasive in the energy sector , which is still dominated by the state holding company ENI and all its subgroups – yet the government is nonetheless subject to constraints. The government has adapted to the IEM, and as Italy is almost wholly dependent on imports there are no domestic interests to oppose a freer energy market.

At the EU level Italy has supported all the IEM measures, but beyond this has played no active role in the process. Domestically it has not restructured the energy sector to any large degree in anticipation of and in conformity with the IEM.

Britain

Britain instituted all the elements of the IEM at the domestic level in its own process of energy privatisation between 1980 and 1995. During this period the state had a clearly defined strategy for the sector, however it was not concerned with energy policy issues but with the ideology and financial effects of privatisation. Against the wishes of energy sector groups the government privatised all public energy companies, starting with oil and gas in 1986. The resulting free market regime was far more radical than that of the IEM. At the EU level the government has actively supported all the IEM measures, and has sought to cultivate the free market aspects of them by opposing everything that hints of institutional build-up.

The following summarises the strategies adopted by the four states towards the IEM:

- France: offensive international strategy
- Germany: defensive international strategy
- UK: offensive domestic strategy
- Italy: defensive domestic strategy

In Putnam's model, the state has a 'gatekeeping' function, but only France has made good use of this. France influenced the IEM proposals in ways that have benefited domestic energy interests, and thus has pursued an offensive international strategy. It was also the architect behind the bilateral agreement on energy with Germany, where it used the IEM to define a mutually beneficial energy arrangement between the two states. Germany attempted to make use of the EU demands to abolish the *Jahrhundertvertrag*, but failed in its pursuit of this at home. Its partial success here is classified as a defensive international strategy. Britain chose to forego the opportunity presented by the IEM and concentrated on domestic restructuring alone, where it clearly pursued an offensive domestic strategy.

Italy ranks at the bottom of the list in terms of pursuing a strategy at either level: the Italian state has not accomplished much in the way of domestic energy policy and has had nothing to lose by accepting all the IEM proposals. It has pursued a defensive domestic strategy in slowly starting the work of restructuring the domestic energy sector to make it more market-responsive.

Putnam pointed out that the 'cleverest' state, or chief negotiator, as he put it, is the one that is able to pursue an offensive international strategy because it can use both the domestic and the international-level negotiations to further its own policy. Domestic opposition could be met by international-level demands that would seem to invalidate the former, and at the international level the government could invoke domestic constraints in a way that would form a basis for the stance it would want to take in a particular case. The making of the IEM is essentially the making of a deregulatory regime, but as has been evident throughout this study, this does not mean that the IEM rules can be taken as given. Only Britain seems to have entertained the notion of 'rolling back the state' in order to let commercial actors take control of the scene. The IEM, however, provided the basis for the struggle over which types of deregulation would result.

The evidence of government strategies at the CEP level in the three cases studied showed that the pursuit of government strategies based on domestic energy interests is not very clear. Attitudes vary and can not be attributed to energy interests alone. East–West European integration and trade possibilities matter, but so do the general views on EU integration and the role of the EU institutions. Unlike the IEM, state interests are not clearly defined and the member states seem to be *followers* in the policy processes rather than activists. There is no correspondence between energy sector interests and the stance taken on the CEP proposals.

EU actors in the energy policy-making process

The Commission has the central role of initiating policy. In the policy-making process it is also the broker of interests and modifier of proposals. Beyond this general role it has, as discussed, played an increasingly important role in the development of the IEM towards the CEP.

The IEM work is mandated by the general internal market concept. The task of the Commission is to ensure that all EU policy conforms to the principles of the internal market. Thus to an extent the contents of the IEM were defined before the Energy Directorate started its work. The mandate was the result of a common position being reached by the European heads of state. However, all the details of the IEM were left to the discretion of the directorate. In other words, it would determine what the problems were and which policy solutions were viable, hence also possibly influencing which positions the states could adopt.

Opposition to the major IEM proposals has been considerable. For gas, the industry interests are singularly opposed to a freer market and this has been echoed by some member states. It is no overstatement to say that the Commission has launched its proposals in the face of very little enthusiasm and support from other actors in the energy sector. The point here is that it is the Commission that has been the main driving force in defining the IEM policy, although some member governments, notably the French, have been active participants. The role of the Commission has been even more pronounced in the case of the CEP. There is no mandate in the White Paper on the internal market for a CEP and no basis for it in the treaties.

Two EU actors are central to understanding the CEP developments: the European Council and the Commission. Both the charter work and the merging of energy and environmental policy resulted from decisions taken by the European Council. However the mandate given to the directorates was very general. The proposal to include a chapter on energy in the revisions to the Treaty on European Union came from the Commission, supported by some member states, including Belgium and Italy. A number of CEP proposals on themes such as an oil sharing mechanism, a general policy for supply security, EU membership of the IEA, the 'upstream' application of competition rules, and so on, came from the Energy Directorate and were often introduced by the energy commissioner at an opportune moment. The suggestion for an EU oil-sharing mechanism, for example, was prompted by the Gulf War.

The case of the European Energy Charter illustrates best how the Commission attained its major policy-making role. After the European Council had concluded that the charter concept forwarded by the Dutch Premier Lubbers was worth further consideration, the arena was in a sense thrown wide open. The EU institutions were not assigned any permanent role in this work, but were asked to make preliminary suggestions. It was entirely undecided where the seat of such a charter would be and who its signatories would be (Lubbers had addressed a constituency consisting of all of Europe and the OECD).

The various member states set out their general views on the charter in the form of non-papers in September–October 1992, and it became evident that the question of which international organisation should be in charge of the charter would not be easily settled. Britain for instance listed almost all the relevant institutions. At the same time the Energy Directorate was conducting informal negotiations with Russia. These took place first in Moscow between Jacques Delors, Frans Andriessen and their Russian counterparts as early as 18–20 July 1990, only one month after the European Council meeting. The energy commissioner conducted the next meeting, again in Moscow, between 11 and 13 September. A third meeting was held in late September, and this time a delegation led by the director-general of the Energy Directorate, C. Maniatopoulos, came from Brussels. *At this meeting all the major aspects of the charter were discussed, partners identified and the basis for the first draft of the charter was agreed.*

The Commission set up a working group, consisting of the DGs for external affairs, energy, and economy, which the proposed a charter conference, to be attended by all European countries. Delors, Lubbers and Kohl mentioned the charter concept at the CSCE summit in Paris in November 1990. A draft text for the charter was discussed at two charter conferences in 1991, where the Commission acted as both initiator and broker. The final charter was signed in December 1991. By that time there was no doubt that the EU would play the major role in the charter proceedings. The EU even advised the CSCE convention in Helsinki in March 1992 that no further initiatives in this area were needed as this might result in work being duplicated.

The discussion that had started in autumn 1990 on which international setting to choose for the charter had proved irrelevant as the Commission had quickly moved to work out the charter contents itself. The negotiations with Russia were already in full swing when the member states began somewhat academically to discuss the issue, so the Commission came to dominate the process. It had a general mandate from the European Council, and the experts from the various directorates started work immediately after the summit in June 1990. Once the groundwork had been accomplished through the negotiations with the Russians, the policy-making process became established as did the role of the Commission in it. From then on it would have been very difficult indeed for a member government or another international organisation to challenge any aspect of the process. In effect the Commission had defined the 'problem', the policy solutions, and which positions the states could have.

The initiating role of the Commission was more important with the CEP than with the IEM. As W. Wallace (1990, p. 215) points out, 'the Commission is no neutral arbiter, but a player with vested interests of its own to promote'. The ambition of the Energy Directorate is clearly to be an important actor in the international energy scene, not to divest itself of influence in the energy sector by simply deregulating it.

'Any practitioner of negotiation well recognises the crucial power of the drafter of the texts', says Wallace (ibid.), and in the agenda building for new policy areas such as environmental policy and a pan-European energy policy this role is extremely important. *Thus the less clearly defined the mandate, the more important the role of the Commission.* In other words, as EU energy policy moved on from the IEM towards a CEP, the importance of the Commission increased.

The Commission has pursued a strategy of its own, aimed at strengthening its formal and informal competences in energy policy. While launching the IEM the Commission continually worked towards a CEP. First, the management of an eventual IEM would require a politically strong Commission. Second, external energy-related events suggested that the EU should design tactics to cope with any similar problems in the future: the Gulf War prompted concern over dependence on imported oil, the demise of the Soviet empire made import dependence on gas a renewed problem, and the alarming extent of polluting energy production and use in Central Europe called for a multilateral response from the EU. Finally, the need to develop virtually all aspects of the energy sectors in the less-developed EU states called for considerable action on the part of the Commission. No one argued – or for that matter believed – that the IEM alone could solve these problems.

The Commission thus had an opportunity to create an energy policy that would imply the transfer of power to itself from the national level. This was done formally in the case of the new competences set out in the Treaty on Political Union: competences in infrastructure, the integration of energy and environmental policy, and intensified of the application of competition legislation. It was done informally through the strengthening of the structural funds – which led to an increased role for the Commission in developing the energy sectors of the less-developed regions – and shaping the Energy Charter.

Notably, all the informal CEP elements have been hidden behind the logic of the IEM. For example, although the development of energy sectors in the south is transitory in the sense that it is aimed at bringing these states up to the standard that exists in the north, CEP-type policies are needed to arrive at an IEM. Likewise the Energy Charter was not presented as a CEP-type policy, but as the extension of the IEM. This has made the evolving EU energy policy acceptable to the member states while the Commission has gradually attained a major policy-making role. It was when they were confronted with a formal transfer of power in the energy area through the treaty revision that most of the states protested.

In summary although the Commission has failed to obtain a formal CEP competence, since 1988 it has come to enjoy both *de jure* and *de facto* powers in EU energy policy.

Theoretical implications: the influence of non-state actors

Above we have seen that EU actors enjoy important formal roles in some issue areas and that the Commission has been able to utilise external events and its formal competence provided that general legitimacy for EU-level policy on the part of the states obtains. In such periods the Commission and the European Court of Justice may 'bypass' the member states and the normal political process of negotiations by intervening directly in cases that can be defined within the remit of the competition legislation.

Having identified what roles it does or can play, we now need to assess the *relative importance* of the part played by the Commission *vis-à-vis* that of the member governments. The predominant theoretical paradigm in this field of study is intergovernmentalism, which allots no independent role to the Commission – measured by the strength of oppositional interests between the states and the Commission. To claim that the Commission exerts an independent force therefore implies that something can be said about its importance relative to that of the member governments. In turn this requires a decision on which criteria we should accept as constituting independent action, and a reasoned opinion on how the role of the Commission can be studied empirically in order to devise a way of determining its impact. The intergovernmentalist perspective holds that the Commission plays no independent role at all, it simply facilitates mediation between states and serves a technical function (Moravcsik, 1993). The Commission is an arena, and in itself an arena can have no influence on policy outcomes. This may however not be so: an arena may also be important. The second perspective is not state-centered in the sense of making assumptions about the primacy of the state as an actor *vis-à-vis* other EU actors. However this perspective is much less specific than the state-centred one and is thus the least theoretically attractive of the two at this stage.

Arena and actor roles of the Commission

We can analytically distinguish between arena and actor roles. An actor influences the output of policy in an independent way, according to the standard understanding of the concept (Sjøstedt, 1977; Underdal, 1992). The criteria for defining someone as an actor must as a minimum include the ability to act at the outset – some degree of autonomy, some independent resources and so on. But also arenas may be politically important. Underdal argues that they may be important for different reasons, and not necessarily in lesser ways than actors (Underdal, 1992).

The Commission's arena roles include its agenda-setting power and its considerable ability to regulate the access of participants. By setting agendas, the Commission may be able to shape states' own agendas: states will take into account EU-level activities and likely strategies when formulating their own strategies. Following this logic, the Commission may not only shape states' agendas but also influence interest formation.

Governments are interested in their reputations and have a desire to be constructive participants in international problem solving. In their study of East-West regimes, Rittberger and Mayer (1993) found the reputational factor to be very important in the political calculations of Russia and Germany. In the EU case, we can expect that a high value is attached to reputation in the sense that no member government wants to be seen as obstructing the policy-making process. This has been particularly important in the post-1985 period, as qualified majority voting means that states can be outvoted. Their general record on fulfilling expectations is important, and since the introduction of qualified majority voting the laggards have become visible – it is much more important than before to be active and cooperative and not to try and halt new policies.

Turning to the actor roles of the Commission, it has formal power to act autonomously in certain policy areas. In competition policy the Commission is formally authorised to act in a way that also has a direct applicability and thus effect in member states. The Competition Directorate intervenes very forcefully in cases where competition is being hindered, and the European Court of Justice has often supported the Commission's moves against companies and member states. Together these two institutions act autonomously. Like a state, the Commission has formal, autonomous powers of action in selected policy areas.

However the degree of its formal power varies according to the issue area. Sometimes a weak or almost non-existent power to act in one issue area may successfully be coupled with competition policy by defining the issue in competition terms, such as when member-states energy companies are monopolies. These became subject to Competition Directorate intervention when energy policy became a subset of internal market issues. The Commission may thus *redefine issues in ways that bend them towards those areas where it yields power*. We have shown that this happened in the post-1985 period. Formal legal powers in one issue area may thus enable the Commission to extend its action to new issues that are being defined in terms of the remit of competition policy.

The actor role is logically different from the arena role. Sometimes the role of the arena may be very powerful, even when this entails no formal power. Institutions playing the arena role may regulate access to the arena and thereby set the agenda. Sometimes the actor role entails extensive political power, be it formal or informal. Thus while it may be analytically useful to distinguish between arena and actor roles, these roles tell us nothing about the wielding of actual power.

When is the Commission at its most powerful?

The Commission has always been busy with something, and its output has grown continuously. However we are interested in the Commission's ability to achieve its own policy goals, whether these are in opposition to or consistent with those of the member states. The empirical evidence strongly indicates that the Commission is able to act under optimal conditions only when there is a major political task to which the member states agree, such as the vision of unity in 1992. In the literature there is agreement that there have been two such periods of Commission activity – the period before the *accords de Luxembourg* in 1966 and the post-1985 period.

We have seen that the Commission can be independently important both as actor and arena, and that it can play an entrepreneurial role, especially during the agenda-setting phase. It can combine its formal powers as enforcer of competition legislation and agenda-setter, with informal roles in the arena or negotiations between the states. The Commission thus has important formal policy-making roles that seem to be activated in periods when EU-level action has been legitimised, as in the post-1985 period.

Given this, the theoretical challenge is to devise a systematic way of studying and assessing the Commission's role, and by implication that of other non-state actors. Which criteria should we employ to decide whether the Commission is an independent actor? One approach to this question is contained in the literature on leadership that applies to the Commission (Rosenthal, 1975; Sandholz, 1993; Vahl, 1992). A number of leadership functions do not depend on the wielding of formal power. Sandholz (1993) uses the concept of entrepreneurial leadership, following *inter alia* Young (1994), who argues that inter-national organisations can exercise leadership in this area in parti-cular. The entrepreneurial leader can promote collective action, which in the case of the Commission consists of proposing policy, mobilising support, shaping agendas, building consensus and broker-ing compromises (Sandholz, 1993, p. 250). In addition there are, according to Sandholz, four conditions under which such leadership will be effective: that the institution's bureaucracy is expert, that its leaders are charismatic, that from the start the institution is endowed with extensive authority, and that there is a 'policy need' on the part of the states. It can be argued that all these conditions existed in the post-1985 period: the internal market filled a 'policy need' on the part of the states, Delors provided personal leadership, the Commission is an expert civil service, and the initial endowment of formal legal powers was very extensive, as in the competition legislation.

These are suggested conditions for effective leadership, but note that Sandholz adds that 'even the presence of all four in a specific situation, however, does not ensure that IO [international organisa-tion] leadership will be effective' (Sandholz, 1993, p. 251). We take this to mean that even if leadership is exercised, it is not being claimed that the international organisation has an independent impact on policy outcomes. Presumably only effective leadership can have such an impact, and even then the leadership literature that has been applied to the Commission is not clear about what the *theoretical claim* is: does effective leadership mean that the Commission has an independent impact on policy outcomes?

Moravcsik asks 'How can you show that the Commission has an independent impact?' (personal correspondence, 1994). Sandholz's implicit criterion for allotting an independent role to the Commission is less rigid than that of Moravcsik, who argues that one either has to pose the historical counterfactual or have a case of opposing interests between the Commission and the states (ibid.) Sandholz uses *time* as a central indication that the Commission has played an independent role: since Commission proposals have consistently been ahead of what the states have developed by way of policy, the Commission is deemed to have had an independent impact on policy (Sandholz, 1993, p. 269). Using this criterion, the Commission had an impact on the national positions on the European Energy Charter.

But does an actor role for the Commission always imply that there must be evidence of independent impact on outcomes? It may very well be that the states *accept the policy definition and derive their interests from the latter*, or there may be *common interests between the states and the Commission*. This is different from the claim that in order to establish whether the Commission has an independent impact we need, for methodological reasons, to have a case of opposing interests between the states and the Commission or be able to establish the historical counterfactual. The problem of establishing the historical counterfactual is formidable (Biersteker, 1993); would there for instance have been an IEM without the Commission's initiative? We think not, but we cannot prove this. When we choose different interests between governments and the Commission as the criterion for assessing whether the Commission has an independent impact, we assume that the interests of the two actors is (1) formed prior to policy-making and (2) oppositional. We also make an assumption about the nature of interests that is quite confining: we assume that interests are about specific cases and narrowly national, and that these interests take precedence over a general approach to integration in a given state. As Burley and Mattli note in a discussion of the ECJ, there are three types of state preference *vis-à-vis* the EU: (1) the support of a system of conflict resolution such as the EC; (2) preferences 'concerning the pace, scope, and degree of European integration' (these two preferences transcend any one particular case), and (3) 'specific economic or political preferences in particular cases' (Burley and Mattli, 1993, p. 184). The method of assessing whether states' interests prevail over those of other EU actors' presupposes that we deal with the third type of interest only. However it is clear that some states place great emphasis on the second category of interests – here Germany comes to mind – while others, such as Britain, are much less concerned about integration as such. Using an analysis of outcomes of interest struggles between case-specific national interests as a criterion for assessing actor importance is only valid in cases where clear-cut interests of the third category are at work.

In cases where government interests cannot be established prior to EU policy-making it is impossible to establish whether government interests prevailed. In cases where we suspect that Commission agenda-setting influences states' definitions of their interests, we need another approach. This approach must be dynamic in order to capture the *interaction* between states and EU-level actors in a given policy process that can be traced in stages: policy initiation and agenda setting, the hammering out of positions and interests, and policy outcomes.

From two-level to multi-level policy analysis: venturing beyond state-centric theory

An increasingly common, and in our view valid, criticism of Putnam's two-level approach is that it oversimplifies by assuming that the 'game' being played between the states and the international organisation, here the EU, is the only important one. Subnational actors as well interest groups matter too:

> Some very basic, and perhaps surprising, features of the emerging political landscape are visible now . . . instead of a neat, two-sided process involving member states and Community institutions, one finds a complex, multilayered decision-making process stretching beneath the state as well as above it, instead of a consistent pattern of policy-making across issue areas, one finds extremely wide and persistent variations. (Marks, 1992, p. 221)

Cameron (1992) rightly remarks that the state-EU interaction is much more complex than a two-level game, and Peters (1992, p. 107) argues that at least three games are being played at any one time: one between the states and the EU, one between the EU institutions in their internal power struggle, and one between the directorates. We would add a fourth: that between the various directorates and interest groups, both subnational and pan-European.

The existence of various types of actor that belong neither to the domestic nor to the EU level poses both an empirical and a logical problem for the two-level model. The empirical evidence of the importance of these actors is growing, and they form direct alliances and linkages with the Commission. Logically they cannot be fitted into the two-level model, which not only presupposes the primacy of state actors, but for this very reason posits a fundamental divide between the domestic and the international levels.

The metatheoretical criticism of the state-centredness of neorealism is by now well-known: neorealism offers a state-centric world view – one must assume that the state is capable of having an interest and a strategy, the state is treated as an unproblematic assumption and thus may easily be reified, and so on (Ashley, 1984; Wendt, 1992; Kratochwil, 1993). In the words of Ashley, 'the state as actor assumption is a metaphysical commitment prior to science and exempted from scientific criticism' (Ashley, 1984, p. 239). One thus has to be able to interpret all actors through the prism of the state. This in turn imposes a certain view of the EU as more· or less 'statelike'. The state ontologically precedes the international system in neorealism and intergovernmentalism. We are so used to thinking in terms of the state in modern political theory that we lack the language for other types of political ordering, as Schmitter (1992) notes.

Our conventional assumptions about the primacy of the state and the existence of a 'national interest' are highly problematic. They tend to reify the state and thus to impose themselves on empirical analysis. The 'two-level' approach opens up the so-called 'black box' of the state. But only when we also open up the 'black box' of EU actors will we be able to make assessments of their independent role and of how they play two- or multilevel games with the states. EU actors, like states, have their 'domestic struggles' within the EU system. However other actors beyond both the nation-state and the EU are gaining in political importance. Their ascendance to power shatters the divide between domestic and international, and thereby logically also the notion of a 'gatekeeping' function. An 'agnostic' approach based on multilevel thinking seems most appropriate for the empirical study of EU actor impact.

The two-level model remains state-centred. It is based on the assumption that the state retains its so-called 'foreign policy prerogative' and is thus able to regulate access to the second level, as well as information about what happens at that level and the feedback of information about the negotiations at the second level to the 'first', domestic level. However the moment we leave the conceptualisation of two levels and start to talk about multiple levels, we also *leave the concept of the state as gatekeeper between the levels. The state, then, is logically only one of several actors.*

But what alternatives do we have if we abandon the assumption of state-centredness? A useful starting point may be to focus on political *processes* (George, 1985) and *policy problems* rather than on actors. It is possible to trace how an issue has come onto the EU agendas: Which actors have been important? What role did external events play? To what extent does the policy problem demand international-level solutions? We can assume that the substance of the policy problem plays a major role in determining which roles states, as opposed to EU actors, will have in its resolution. This is, incidentally, a rephrasing of the old functionalist argument that integration is problem-driven. However this is by no means an automatic process: actors do not accept some sort of functional classification of problems and on this basis 'assign' them to the EU or the nation-state for resolution, as ideally the principle of subsidiarity would have it. Nonetheless this does not mean that the substance of policy is unimportant to the determination of actor impact on the policy process.

Furthermore, by focusing on process rather than on formal actors we do not have to assume that formal power implies actual power and that actors have fixed interests prior to the commencement of the policy-making process. The formal actor role may, as stated, have little to do with the actual wielding of political power. For example non-governmental organisations may be much more powerful in the agenda-setting phase of an international negotiation than governments, despite the fact that they may not have any formal role.

Thus in order to go beyond the focus on actors first and interests second, a viable approach may be to look at the negotiating process itself: at the definition of the problem, the setting of the agenda, the inclusion/exclusion of participants and so on. This allows the importance of the *stages* of policy-making to be analysed, and this may be a key to determining the importance of various actors.

Governments probably matter more in the negotiation phase than in the agenda-setting phase, which is characterised by the overriding importance of problem-definition rather than by the specification of actors' interests, which belongs to the subsequent negotiation phase. If the analysis starts with the policy problem rather than actors' interests, a fruitful analysis can be made of what happens in the agenda-setting phase. The fact that the Commission plays an almost exclusive role here is known to be important, but we lack adequate criteria with which to evaluate the importance of this phase compared with the negotiation phase, where an outcome is arrived at. What is interesting to determine here is the extent to which states' and other actors' interests are influenced by the Commission's agenda setting. It could be fruitful to combine a processual analysis of agenda setting with an actor-based analysis of the negotiation phase.

Among several interesting theoretical vantage points from which to develop such an analytical framework is the literature on regime formation and regime impact. Young (1994) has developed theories on the impact of various types of actors in the various stages of international negotiations, pointing out that in the agenda-setting phase the role of ideas, knowledge and so on may play a large role as opposed to the traditional notion of a national interest. Governance systems may be created without formal state actors, and the power of ideas may be as important as material power. In the prenegotiation phase, when the agenda is set, the power of ideas and knowledge matters, whereas in the subsequent negotiation phase, instrumental and structural interests matter more, Young argues. Young also discusses the development and impact of international regimes. They are usually not formal actors and consequently do not possess formal power instruments, unlike the Commission. Nonetheless they can be shown to have an impact, both in terms of compliance and in their importance as agenda setters. We may assume that the Commission's formal power strengthens its agenda-setting power: other actors need to pay attention to this as they are 'stuck in the game' as it were – they cannot exit but are legally bound by the *acquis*.

In summary, a breakdown of the policy process into stages seems necessary for an assessment of relative actor importance as well as for when and whence interests are generated.

Theoretical conclusions

There is such a great EU-role variation between issue areas that there can hardly be a general theory of the states–EU relationship. This is illustrated by the gap between the 'political union' and the reality of foreign policy among the member states, which is not even coordinated. It is therefore likely that the *substance* of the policy area plays a major role in determining which roles EU-level actors will play. In areas where there are clear international policy consequences, for example environmental policy, the potential for international governance is large. In other areas, where geopolitical interests are already entrenched, there will be a clear-cut definition of interests from the outset. Energy is an example of this. Because the EU has important legal tools with which to enforce legislation, its actor role in 'weak' issue areas may be strengthened by the use of these tools and by linkage politics. However as we have argued, the latter is only possible in periods when EU-level activity has been legitimised.

If we start with the substance of the policy area and trace the process of policy-making from agenda setting to outcome, we avoid the problem of state-centredness and follow an unprejudiced approach to actor roles and actor impact. Governments may turn out to be dominant in most cases, but occasionally we may find that EU-level actors are surprisingly important in defining the agenda, the stakes and the outcome. We must of course specify hypotheses about the role of the various actors at the outset, and if possible delineate the domestic 'game' being played by that the state as well as the 'intra-Commission games', where there will almost always be conflict between directorates and between the Commission and other EU-level actors. We may find that actors' interests are shaped by the agenda and the negotiations, that learning occurs, and that states choose to support solutions that go beyond their 'national interest'.

In summary, a multilevel actor approach to the study of integration seems increasingly appropriate, combined with a processual analysis of the various stages of decision-making. The often implicit assumption of state-centredness precludes both the consideration of the importance of the policy problem and that of other actors. This critique leads to the conclusion that it is high time that intergovernmentalism – in its traditional as well as its 'improved', two-level form – should be abandoned for the sake of conceptually richer developments of integration theory.

Conclusion: The Future of EU Energy Policy

In this book we have seen that energy policy in the EU has developed from humble beginnings, even though two of the three founding treaties concerned energy. It was only with the advent of the internal market, which also came to include energy, that a policy in this area gradually emerged. The Commission started with an ambitious programme to deregulate the energy sector and dismantle energy monopolies, but only a few of these proposals were eventually adopted. The internal market in energy was slow to materialise. The most controversial directive – electricity transit liberalisation – took six years to negotiate, and then was only adopted in a modified form as a compromise between the wishes of Germany and France. Nonetheless the process of creating an IEM was significant and persistent despite the opposition of some member states and many interest groups.

The Commission's main strength lay in the member states' commitment to the internal market, in its legal procedures that prescribed majority acceptance of internal market proposals (Article 100a of the Single European Act), and in the competition legislation that was being increasingly applied to the energy sector for the first time in the EU's history. In its most active period (between 1985 and about 1992) the Commission quite creatively capitalised on the many 'windows of opportunity' that were opened by external events. For example it tried to forge a policy for Eastern and Central Europe, with energy as one of the main components, and developed the same type of policy for the Mediterranean area, to mention but two. It likewise tried to establish a formal competence for energy in both the Treaty on European Union and the new treaty that resulted from the intergovernmental conference that started in 1996.

151

Differences between member states in energy policy persisted, although from 1985–95 there was an important degree of convergence on market liberalisation as a policy paradigm. However, France its energy companies wanted to retain a clear public service function, whereas Britain tried to have a free market in energy adopted at the EU level.

In the period primarily considered in this book (1985–95) EU energy policy was able to develop not so much because of external 'threats' such as actual or potential supply disruption, but more as part of a common programme – the internal market – and its ideology of deregulation. Deregulation is a typical EU policy, and here the Commission and the European Court of Justice have their strengths. These factors together go a long way towards explaining why the Commission was able to construct elements of a common energy policy while vigorously pursuing the IEM. However, as noted in the preceding chapters, the activity of both the Commission and the Court waned after about 1990–92. This was a general phenomenon, visible to the political observer but also measurable in terms of the number of new draft directives and cases initiated by the Competition Directorate and the Court. The pace of activity lessened, as did the boldness of proposals.

In the Commission's Green Paper on energy, published in late 1995, the tone was cautious when its own role was discussed, and in its subsequent White Paper (1996) it was careful not to suggest new roles and competences for the EU institutions in the energy field. Nonetheless the goal of establishing a common policy has not been abandoned by the Commission.

What are we to make of this? Will EU energy policy wane in line with the reduction in support for general EU policies since the inception of the internal market? Will the momentum that has been built up regarding a common energy policy towards Eastern and Southern Europe be lost? Will national interests continue to prevail in all further work on the IEM? Will the environment become neglected in energy policy, as is the case in most member countries and largely in the EU as a whole? Let us reflect on the future of energy policy in the EU and Europe:

Firstly we need to remember that the relative power between EU-level actors and state actors is not constant, but varies with issue area, from state to state, and with the general climate for integration. The 1985–92 period was one of extraordinary optimism about the EU's role, and the internal market provided state actors with a common project whose ideology they all shared, although they differed in particulars, as was evident in the struggles over the IEM. This situation provided the Commission with an excellent opportunity to further its own role and develop a comprehensive energy policy – as we have seen many times in this book. External events also provided very good opportunities – there was a need for policy leadership *vis-à-vis* Eastern and Central Europe, and the Commission took this and other opportunities to develop a common energy policy. The question to be answered in this period of less integrative enthusiasm is: what remains of policy power at the EU-level in this issue area? Will it wane with reduced state support, or will it stay? Will the EU institutions be able to take advantage of opportunities that present themselves in the future?

This is a vexing and challenging question in current research on the EU and its importance as a political actor. From many empirical studies we know that EU-level actors played a major role in this period. But when we study the role of the Commission or the Court in negotiations with the states over one issue only, we often get a static picture. As we have seen in this book, the intergovernmentalist perspective is useful, yet not optimal if we want to see how the Commission has developed its role over time.

In studying the role of the Commission, intergovernmentalism is far too simplistic and constraining in its actor conceptualisation, and by mainly focusing on state actors the emphasis is on just one bargain or policy event at a particular time.

But political decisions, although the outcome of bargaining among state interests, tend to have unintended consequences, generate 'sunk costs' and evolve in unanticipated ways. EU institutions and actors play major roles in interpreting and practising agreed rules and norms and in implementing decisions, and tend to utilise the slack control member states have over them in day-to-day affairs to their own organisation's advantage. Actors such as the Commission thus attain their influence in a variety of ways, based on resources beyond formal powers, and they outlive the initial interests that created them. They have a life of their own that can only be seen by studying what they do with formal decisions over time: how does the Commission interpret, apply and implement decisions taken mainly by states?

As we also have seen in this book, the influence of non-state actors such as the Commission is best studied over time. In studies of formal intergovernmental negotiations such as a treaty revisions, the only formal actors are the states. But over time the Commission interprets the resultant treaty and applies its conditions. Its power is thus less visible than that of the states, and is best shown by looking at how the EU has evolved. However most studies of the Commission's role look at one or two negotiating situations – 'bargains' – and at the relative influence of various actors at a given point in time. But the Commission's influence may best be unearthed if we adopt an approach that allows us to see how it has used its formal and informal resources to expand its own role.

There are several reasons why states cannot wield much influence in the intervals between major intergovernmental bargaining: exiting the EU is becoming increasingly difficult; the evolving *acquis* is imposing constraints; states do not always maintain long-term interests, for instance these may change with a change of government; preferences may differ from those held when the treaties were negotiated; and as a rule there are unintended consequences of decisions. The Commission is in an almost ideal position to utilise these factors to its own advantage – as has been shown in the preceding chapters, it can forge issue linkages, define new policies, group policies into areas where it has formal powers and exercise leadership.

This perspective on the Commission's role lets us study how it uses its formal and informal powers over time – for instance when it shapes new documents such as the Energy Charter or tries to form a comprehensive policy towards Eastern and Central Europe. We now have a number of empirical studies of the Commission's role in various policy areas in the post-1985 period, but these have not been treated in the same analytical way and are therefore difficult to compare. However they note that rules and decisions laid down by the states usually develop in ways unanticipated by these same states and that both the Commission and the Court expertly observe the general political climate regarding support for EU-level policy making.

In this analysis we have seen how the Commission has interpreted the mandate given by the states to the IEM in ways that the states have sometimes opposed. Also, we have seen how the IEM has been used as the basis for developing a CEP, or at least elements of one. It is thus clear that the Commission has been active in the field of energy. However, will it be able to continue to its activity in the future? An example relating to how the energy commissioner perceived his power in 1996 may be give an indication of this.

The Energy Commissioner quite often threatened to take states to the European Court of Justice over contentious issues, especially if they were dragging their feet on implementation of the IEM. Later, however, there was much less of this kind of talk. Instead the energy commissioner stressed the states' commitment to completing the internal market, including the IEM, and ceased to confront the states directly. In the long-drawn-out negotiations over the electricity transit directive, rather than using his old threat of taking states to court, Papoutsis merely stated that unless an agreement were reached at the extraordinary energy ministers meeting before the Florence summit in June 1996 he would ask the summit itself to pronounce on the matter. This was a much weaker threat than invoking Article 90,3 of the EEC, which allows the Commission to push through directives without consulting the European Parliament or the Council. Earlier both Papoutsis and Commission President Jacques Santer had used this threat repeatedly in an attempt to break the electricity transit stalemate. Papoutsis acknowledged that this weaker move reflected a weaker position for the Commission: 'It would be a very difficult situation . . . I would prefer not to go down this route . . . we could send states to the court but we would create conflicts between member states and the Commission and I think it would have a very bad effect on public opinion' (*EC Energy Monthly*, February 1996).

This example shows that the Commission's power is precarious. It has to take into account the general political climate, and must be careful not to propose policies that have little support among the member states. Now that the internal market is in place and new issues are on the agenda, it has to look carefully for new opportunities.

The conclusion must be that the Commission has been clearly restrained from using both its formal and informal competences in energy, as in other policy areas, in the post-1992 period. However it may still be able to capitalise on the basis for an IEM and a CEP that was built up in the 'golden' period from 1985 to 1992, especially if external events demand a policy response.

What types of opportunity are likely to open up in the energy field? Put differently, which challenges to energy policy will persist, arise or disappear? The Commission's White Paper on energy policy (1996) posits three major challenges in the energy field in Europe: supply dependency, the environment and the need for an open market in energy. These three pillars will form the core of an EU energy policy;

and one could add, of national energy policies as well. We shall briefly look at how these issues may develop in the future:

Supply security is a recurrent problem in Europe, and is at the core of the EU's energy initiatives in Eastern and Central Europe and the Maghreb region. As Europe is becoming increasingly dependent on natural gas, its dependence on gas from the CIS is growing. In addition there is the continuing problem of supply dependence on Middle Eastern oil. The increasing use of gas throughout Europe has come at a time when supplies are politically more insecure than they have been for a long time: the dissolution of the Soviet Union meant an end to central control and central energy bargaining with the West – a system regarded by energy actors as very efficient and very stable. What has replaced it is a system of overlapping but independent jurisdictions. On occasion disputes have broken out between the new states over transit through each others' territory, and there are few common rules for dispute settlement. In a business as conservative as the European gas industry this has been bad news. What is required are long-term contracts, as well as a great deal of trust and confidence in the sellers, transporters and producers.

The EU developed both the Energy Charter and its policy of establishing energy centres and energy programmes in Eastern Europe as a partial response to these problems. An energy centre was opened in Sofia in the Black Sea region as part of a strategy to deal with potential supply interruptions; or rather to try to prevent them from happening. The centre, where 12 states and the Commission are partners – Albania, Armenia, Azerbaijan, Bulgaria, Georgia, Greece, Moldova, Romania, Russia, Turkey and the Ukraine – was opened by the Energy Directorate in 1996. The main aims of the centre are to promote large-scale energy cooperation in the region, to promote the Energy Charter and apply its conditions, and to work on making energy investment from the West attractive. The region is a key transit area for Russian gas.

Likewise the Commission has been keen to develop a strategy for energy cooperation with the Magreb, as more and more gas is being piped to the EU from Algeria, which remains a political hot-house. The EU way is to find practical types of cooperation in energy, transport and industry, not only to secure existing supplies of gas but also to mould politico-economic cooperation in general. The first ministerial meeting on this 'Euro-Mediterranean partnership' was held in Barcelona in early 1996; the second conference devoted to energy cooperation took place in Trieste later in the same year.

It is hard to evaluate the effect and importance of these kinds of initiative. Supply contracts exist between individual states or consortia of states, and the EU does not really have a role in energy trade, even if it has a strong ambition to develop such a role. The 1996 White Paper speaks about the role the Commission should have in coordinating national positions, but not about any role beyond that. There is probably little political will in any member state for a more active role, and it seems unlikely that the EU will attain such a role because the IEA already monitors and coordinates member states' supply interruption policy. There is little if any reason to duplicate this work.

Turning to the *environment*, this policy area will remain high on all states' agendas, and also on that of the EU. But little of substance has happened in terms of integrating energy and environmental policy. The saga of the carbon tax in the EU has been going on for a long time, but not very successfully from the point of view of the Commission. Although the commissioner responsible for taxation, Mario Monti, argued that 'the use of economic instruments in the service of the environment is one theme where the introduction of measures becomes increasingly likely with each passing year' (*Europe Energy*, June 1996), in 1996 there is little indication that the reluctant member states will change their attitude towards an EU-wide carbon tax. The argument over the need for fiscal harmonisation because of the internal market and the planned single currency has been intensified by the Commission throughout 1996, but to little avail. The carbon tax remains extremely controversial among member states and energy companies, and also in relation to the cooperation with OPEC in the Gulf Cooperation Council, where 'at each meeting the Gulf countries reiterate their opposition to the tax' (ibid., p. 4). Thus there is a direct contradiction between the EU's desire to develop good relations with OPEC and the wish to see a carbon tax imposed. Also, member states have been so divided on this issue that in 1996, after several years of stalemate on the original tax proposal, they could not even agree about giving the Commission a mandate to propose a new tax policy. Thus the imposition of a carbon tax has become even more uncertain. It should also be mentioned that almost no EU member states are enthusiastic about a climate policy, and few states have any hope of reaching the stabilisation target for carbon emissions agreed in Rio in 1992.

Therefore it is hardly surprising that 'new ideas and solutions have to be found to further integrate energy and environmental policies', according to a Commission report issued in 1996 as an evaluation of the Fifth Environmental Action Programme – 'Towards Sustainability' – which spans the period 1992–2000 (*EC Energy Monthly*, 26 February 1996). The programme outlined how environmental concerns must be integrated into various areas of policy, among them energy. But energy is one of the main areas where next to nothing has happened, concludes the report. Despite having the necessary technology, low energy prices have not provided an incentive for lower consumption. Instead energy demand is forecast to rise by about 22 per cent between 1990 and 2010, while the outlook for reducing CO_2 emissions through political measures seems equally distant. In 1996 the Commission had to fight very hard for a five-year extension of the SAVE energy efficiency programme.

Thus while the political rhetoric about the need for supranational environmental policies continues among the member states, there is little political will to do something that will incur a cost. A legal competence for a common environmental policy exists in the Treaty on European Union, but the Commission lacks the support to do much in this area unless a major window of opportunity opens up. Ironically this might have to be a major environmental disaster. The day-to-day politics on the environment lacks incentives and strength. This being said, it is very clear that environmental problems have an international dimension that requires them to be solved through international cooperation, and in this field there is no other political forum in Europe. The EU has its EEB (European Environmental Bureau), consisting of all member states and some non-member states, and it possesses relatively strong policy instruments in the area. These may be activated if a pressing political problem emerges in relation to the environment in Europe, or if the Commission proposes an environmental policy that appeals to the member states. It is quite possible that in a major crisis, for instance another nuclear accident in Eastern or Central Europe, the EU may emerge as the leading political actor in responding to this. However this will require considerable political leadership on the part of the Commission, something it has lacked in the post-1992 period. Neither of the two directorates in question – Energy and Environment – seems to possess sufficient weight that to provide the necessary leadership. One would have to count on the Commission president, backed by some of the main member states.

Perhaps the potential source of strength lies exactly here: member states will eventually need a common policy and a 'level playing field' to respond to common environmental problems. This is more likely to spur integration in energy–environmental policies than any new initiative by the Commission. Papoutsis' logic that 'an energy chapter [in the new treaty] would not give the Commission more powers over the sector, but would ensure that energy carries a similar weight to those of the environment or fiscal policy' (ibid., 26 February 1996) is not likely to convince the member states. When it comes to the environment and energy, only strong external stimuli are likely to result in a common EU policy. The incentives for this are absent in 'normal' times, when costly environmental policies are opposed by both market and political actors. Only strong popular pressure triggered by a real or perceived crisis or an imminent problem will force controversial policies through at the EU or the national level. When the environment is not in dramatic focus, there is little to drive the political process. Environmental non-governmental organisations are weak compared with energy companies, something that is reflected in studies of the impact of such groups when lobbying in the EU. When policy proposals become concrete the industry tends to activate itself and exert a disproportionate influence, but at times when environmental matters are confined to political rhetoric the really powerful actors in the industry do not involve themselves. At the moment the so-called 'voluntary measures' prevail at the EU level and in member states as the political solution to the impasse over the integration of environmental and energy policy.

The third area in the EU's energy policy portfolio is the continued work towards the completion of the *internal energy market*. The record here is uneven – from the easy acceptance of some directives to the extremely slow and difficult negotiations over electricity transit. The next task is to open the gas market to more competition. This is likely to be much more difficult to bring about than the equivalent electricity directive. Papoutsis declares that 'the same people who press for the internal market in electricity are much more reticent when it comes to gas' (ibid., 26 February 1996). With much less general enthusiasm for EU-level policies, one can safely predict that there will be many odds against the Commission meeting with success here. Yet there is a trend towards increased market opening and competition in energy in general, and it may be impossible to resist this in the long run.

The compromise on the electricity transit was over free market versus public service functions. France wanted to retain its distribution monopolies, while the Commission, Germany and Britain were against it. Although the Commission could have pushed through its proposal by insisting on majority voting, it chose not to do so. As suggested earlier, this indicates that the Commission does not perceive it to be wise to antagonise member states over this issue at this time, whereas it did push through a vote in 1990 when there was a stalemate over Germany's opposition to modified open access to gas transit. The eventual compromise over this directive shows that there are important national differences in market structures, energy policies and market philosophies – from Britain's extremely free-market orientation to France's insistence on retaining energy companies in public hands. These differences are not likely to disappear unless the Commission exerts a certain amount of pressure, and in the later half of the 1990s it is more uncertain than ever that it will be able to do this. Much depends on developments on energy policy in the member countries, and less on developments at the EU level.

Guide to Further Reading

There are no book-length studies of EU energy policy, but various articles and reports do deal with the topic.

On the European gas market and the implications the internal energy market has for the latter, see Jonathan Stern, *European Gas Markets: Challenge and Opportunity in the 90s* (London: RIIA, 1992) and a joint report by the RIIA and the SPRU entitled *A Single European Market in Energy* (Sussex: RIIA/SPRU, 1989). The latter consists of empirical analyses of the various energy types and the market implications of energy policy developments in the EU. Then there is Francis MacGowan's report on electricity market changes as a consequence of the single energy market, *The Struggle for Power in Europe: Competition and Regulation in the Electricity Industry* (London: RIIA, 1993).

Svein Andersen has written a very good report on the energy charter and the 'upstream' licensing directive under the auspices of the Norwegian Research Council s PETRO-programme, *Europeification of Policy-Making: The Case of Petroleum Policy* (Oslo: Norwegian School of Management, 1996).

These above studies are aimed at an audience interested in energy questions, in essence those that work in the energy industry. The emphasis is thus empirical, on implications for the market structure of various energy types.

The current author has published several articles in anthologies on the EU single energy market and its implications for Norwegian energy interests, (including 'The EC Policy-Making Process in the Field of Energy: An Analysis with a View to Norwegian Interests' and 'Selling Norwegian Gas: from Collective Domestic Strategy Towards Individual Downstream Integration?', both of which appear in *Norwegian Gas in the New Europe: How Politics shape Markets*, (Oslo: Vett og Viten, 1991); 'Norwegian Gas and the EC: Implications of an Internal Energy Market', in H. Bergesen, and A. Sydnes, *Naive Newcomer or Shrewd Salesman? Norway a major Oil and Gas Exporter*, (Oslo: FNI, 1990). All these studies are aimed at an energy policy audience rather than a general audience interested in European integration.

A theoretically interesting article is Stephen Padgett's 'The Single European Energy Market: The Politics of Realization', *JCMS*, vol. xxx, no. 1 (March 1992), which examines German and French energy policy *vis-à-vis* the EU. This article is the only one that has been written on the subject within a more general theoretical framework, viz. intergovernmentalism.

The main sources of information on the empirical development of EU energy policy are the industrial periodicals, notably *EC Energy Monthly*, and

161

Europe Energy, both of which deal specifically with the EU. The Commission publishes a useful periodical entitled *Energy in Europe*. *EuropeEnvironment* provides information on the development of environmental policy in the EU, and this is also highly relevant for energy policy. Among the periodicals that are important to study of the development of the energy sector in Europe in general and in Eastern and Central Europe are *European Energy Report* and *East European Energy Report*. The best source for the general policy process of the EU is clearly the news bulletin *Europe: Agence internationale d'information pour la presse*, which is published daily.

Academic books that are important for understanding the dynamic of the internal market process in general as well as other policy areas include Sandholz' detailed study of the telecommunications sector, *High-Tech Europe: the Politics of International Cooperation* (Berkeley, CA: University of California Press, 1992) and Tsoulakis' study of *The New European Economy: the Politics and Economics of Integration* (Oxford: Oxford University Press, 1993). The comprehensive study by Neill Nugent of the policy-making process and EU institutions, *The Government and Politics of the European Union*, 3rd edn, (London: Macmillan, 1994) is the best guide to general aspects of the functioning of the EU. Among the academic periodicals that offer both empirical analyses and theoretical discussions, the *Journal of Common Market Studies* is the most useful. There are also articles on the development of the various policy areas in various journals, but so far few book-length studies.

References

Books, academic articles and reports

Andersen, S. (1996) *The Europeification of Policy-Making: The Case of Petroleum Policy* (Oslo: Norwegian School of Management, research report for the PETRO-programme).

Archer, C. (1994) *Organizing Europe: The Institutions of Integration* (London: Edward Arnold).

Ashley, R. K. (1984) 'The Poverty of Neorealism', *International Organization*, vol. 38, no. 2 (Spring).

Aspinall, M. (1995) 'International Integration or Internal Politics? Anatomy of a Single Market Measure', *Journal of Common Market Studies*, vol. 33, no. 4 (December).

Autzeichnung: Intensivierung der eüropeischen Zusammenarbeit im Energisektor (1990) Bundesministerium der Wirtschaft, Autumn, 1990, Non-Paper.

Bennet, G. (1988) 'A Common Environmental Policy for a Common Market?', in *The Environmental Policy in a Market Economy* (Holland: Pudoc Wageningen).

Bergesen, H. O. (1990), *EFs klimapolitikk* (Oslo: FNI).

Beyme, K. von (1983) *The Political System of Germany* (Aldershot: Gower).

Biersteker, T. (1993) 'Constructing Historical Counterfactuals to Assess the Consequences of International Regimes: The Global Debt regime and the Course of the Debt-Crisis in the 1980s', in V. Rittberger, assisted by P. Mayer (ed.), *Regime Theory and International Relations* (Oxford: Clarendon Press).

Black, R. A. (1977), 'Plus Ça Change, Plus C'est le meme Chose: Nine Governments in Search of a Common Energy Policy', in H. Wallace, W. Wallace and C. Webb, *Policy-making in the European Community* (London: John Wiley and Sons).

Bressand, A. and K. Nicolaides (1990) 'Regional Integration in a Networked World Economy', in W. Wallace, *The Dynamics of European Integration* (London: Pinter).

British Petroleum (1991) *Statistical Review of World Energy*.

Budge, I. and P. McKay (1983) *The New British Political System: Government and Society in the 1980s* (London: Longman).

Bulmer, S. (1983) 'Domestic Policies and EC Policy-Making', *Journal of Common Market Studies*, vol. XXI, no. 4 (June).

Bulmer, S. and W. Paterson (1996) 'Germany in the EU: Gentle Giant or Emergent Leader?', *International Affairs*, January.

Bundesministerium für Umweltfragen (1990) *Umweltpolitik*, Report (Germany: Bundesministerium für Umweltfragen).

Bundesministerium für Umweltspolitik (1990), *Zielvorstellung für eine erreichbare Reduktion der CO₂ Emissionen* (Germany: Bundesministerium für Umweltspolitik).

Bundesministerium für Wirtschaft (1983) *Die Entwicklung der Gaswirtschaft in der Bundesrepublik Deutschland im Jahre 1983* (Bonn: Bundesministerium für Wirtschaft).

Burley, A.- M. and W. Mattli (1993) 'Europe before the Court: A Political Theory of Legal Integration', *International Organization*, vol. 47.

Cameron, D. (1992) 'The 1992 Initiative: Causes and Consequences', in A. Sbragia *Europolitics: Institutions and Policy-Making in the 'New' European Community* (Washington, DC: Brookings Institution).

Cecchini, P. *et al.* (1988) *Europa 1992: Realiseringen av det indre marked* (Oslo: Dagens Næringslivs forlag).

Clark, J. (1990) *The Political Economy of World Energy: A 20th Century Perspective* (New York: Harvester Wheatsheaf)

Cohen, B. J. (1990) 'The Political Economy of International Trade' *International Organization*, vol. 44, no. 2 (Spring).

Cooper, R. C. (1968) *The Economics of Interdependence: Economic Policy in the Atlantic Community* (New York: McGraw-Hill).

Cowles, M. G. (1995) 'Setting the Agenda for a New Europe. The ERT and EC 1992', *Journal of Common Market Studies*, vol. 33, no. 4 (December).

Dahl-Martinsen, K. (1990) *Naturgass i øst-Europa* (Oslo: FNI).

Dalton, R. (1989) *Politics in West Germany* (Glenview, Ill: Scott, Foresman & Co.).

Davis, J. D. (1984) *Blue Gold: The Political Economy of Natural Gas* (London, Allen & Unwin).

Dehousse, B. (1992) 'Integration v. Regulation? On the Dynamics of Regulation in the EC', *Journal of Common Market Studies*, vol. xxx, no. 4 (December).

Dekker, W. (1990) *Europa 1990* (Eindhoven: Philips).

Deubner, C. (1979) 'The Expansion of West-German Capital and the founding of Euratom', *International Organization*, vol. 33, no. 2 (Spring).

D'Herbes J. and J. Touscoz (n.d.) *L'Europe et la coopération internationale dans le domaine énergétique. Actes du colloque internationale organisé par l'Institut pour le développement de la coopération internationale.*

Energierecht (1980), 5th edn (Essen: Textsammlung).

Estrada, J. *et al.* (1988) *Natural Gas: Markets, Organizations, and Politics* (London: Francis Pinter).

European Environmental Bureau (1990) *Memorandum to the Italian Presidency from the EEB* (European Environmental Bureau).

European Union (*see separate section below*).

Evans, P., D. Rueschmeyer and T. Skocpol (1985) *Bringing the State Back In* (Cambridge: Cambridge University Press).

Farneti, P. (1985) *The Italian Party System, 1945–1980* (London: Pinter).

Feigenbaum, B. (1985) *The Politics of Public Enterprise: Oil and the French State* (Princeton, N.J., Princeton University Press).

Fischer, W. and P. Lundgren (1975) 'The Recruitement and Training of Administrative Personnel', in C. Tilly, *The Formation of Nation-States in Western Europe* (Princeton, NJ: Princeton University Press).

Garrett, G. (1992) 'International Cooperation and Individual Choice: The EC's Internal Market', *International Organization*, 46 (Spring).

George, A. and T. McKeown (1985) 'Case Studies and Theories of Organizational Decision-Making', *Advances in Information Processing in Organizations*, vol. 2.

George, S. (1991a), *Politics and Policy in the EC* (Oxford: Oxford University Press).

George, S. (1991b) 'The Domestic Politics Approach: The Case of British Policy in the EC', ECPR Workshops, University of Essex, March.

George, S. (1992) 'Intergovernmentalism, Supranationalism and the Future Development of the EC', paper presented at the ECPR's Inaugural Pan-European Conference, Heidelberg 16–20 September.

German Enquete Commission (1990), *Protecting the Earth*, A Status Report with Recommendations for a New Energy Policy (Bonn: Ministry of Environment).

Gilpin, R. (1987) *The Political Economy of International Relations* (Princeton, NJ: Princeton University Press).

Grubb, M. (1991) 'Greenhouse Responses in the UK and EC: Will Britannia waive the Rules?, in M. Grubb *et al.* (eds) *Energy Policies and the Greenhouse Effect*, vol. 2 (London: RIIA).

Haas, E. (1990) *When Knowledge is Power* (Berkeley: University of California Press).

Haas, P. (1993) 'Epistemic Communities and the Dynamics of International Environmental Cooperation', in V. Rittberger and P. Mayer, *Regime Theory and International Relations* (Oxford: Clarendon Press, 1993).

Haigh, N. and D. Baldock (1989) *Environmental Policy and 1992* (London: HMSO).

Hall, P. (1986) *Governing the Economy: The Policies of State Intervention in Britain and France* (Cambrige: Polity Press).

Hatch, M. (1991) 'Corporatism, Pluralism and Post-Industrial Politics: Nuclear Energy Policy in West Germany', *West European Politics*, vol. 14, no. 1, (Jan.)

Heclo, H. (1974) *Modern Social Policies in Britain and Sweden: From Relief to Income Maintenance* (London: Yale University Press).

Heritier, A. *et al.* (1994) *Die Veranderung von Staatlichkeit in Europa: Ein Regulativer Wettbewerb- Deutschland, Grossbritannien, Frankreich* (Opladen: Leske und Budrich).

Hoffman, S. (1982) 'Reflections on the Nation-State in Western Europe Today', *Journal of Common Market Studies*, vol. XXI, nos 1, 2 (Sept./Dec).

Holland, S. (1973) *The State as Entrepreneur* (New York: International Arts and Science Press).

Huelshoff, M. and T. Pfeiffer (1991) 'Environmental Policy in the EC: Neo-functionalist Sovereignty Transfer or Neo-Realist Gate-Keeping?', *International Journal*, vol. XLVII, no. 2 (Winter).

International Energy Agency (IEA) (1994) *Energy Policies in the IEA Countries* (Paris: OECD).

International Energy Agency (IEA) (1994a) *Climate Change Policy Initiatives*, vol. 1 (Paris: OECD).

International Energy Agency (IEA) (1994b) *Natural Gas Transportation: Organisation and Regulation* (Paris: OECD).

Jachtenfuchs, M. (1990) 'The EC and the Problem of the Ozone Layer', *Journal of Common Market Studies*, vol. XXVIII, no. 3 (March).

Jacops, D. M. and J. Stewart-Clark (1991) *Competition Law in the EC* (London: Kogan Page).

Katzenstein, P. (1978) *Between Power and Plenty: Foreign Economic Policies of Advanced Industrial States* (Madison: Wisconsin University Press).

Keohane, R. and Hoffman, S. (eds) (1991) *The New European Community: Decision-Making and Institutional Change* (Boulder: Westview Press).

Kramer, S. (1976) 'State Power and the Structure of International Trade', *World Politics,* vol. 28 (April).

Kraemer, R. A. (1992), *Assessment of the Fourth and Fifth Environmental Action Programme* (Bonn: Institut für Europäische Umweltpolitik).

Kratochwil, F. (1993) 'The Embarassment of Change: Neo-realism as the Science of *Realpolitik* without Politics', *Review of International Studies,* 19.

Kuster, G. H. (1974) 'Germany', in R. Vernon (ed.), *Big Business and the State: Changing Relations in Western Europe* (Cambridge, Mass: Harvard University Press).

Lake, P. (1988) *Power, Protection, and Free Trade: International Sources of US Commercial Strategy, 1987–1939* (Ithaca, NY: Cornell University Press).

Laurson, F. (1991) 'Environment', in H. Wallace (ed.), *The Wider Western Europe: Reshaping the EC/EFTA Relations* (London: Pinter).

Laux, J. K. and M. A. Holst (1988) *State Capitalism: Public Enterprise in Canada* (Ithaca, NY: Cornell University Press).

Lodge, J. (1989) 'EC Policy Making: Institutional Considerations, in J. Lodge (ed.), *The EC and the Challenge of the Future* (London: Pinter).

Louis, J. V. (1990) *The Community Legal System* (Luxembourg: Office for Official EC Publications).

Lucas, N D. (1977) 'The Role of Institutional Relationships in French Energy Policy', *International Relations* vol. 5 (November).

Lucas, N D. (1985), 'West German Energy Policy', in N D. Lucas, *West European Energy Policies: A Comparative Study of the Influence of Institutional Change on the Structure of Technological Change* (Oxford: Clarendon Press).

Ludlow, P. (1991) 'The European Commission', in R. Keohane and S. Hoffman, *The New European Community: Decision-Making and International Change* (Boulder, Col: Westview Press)

Majone, G. (1990) *Deregulation or Reregulation? Regulatory Reform in Europe and the US* (London: Pinter).

Majone, G. (1994) 'The Rise of the Regulatory State in Europe', unpublished manuscript (Florence: EUI).

Marks, G. (1992) 'Structural Policy in the EC', in A. Sbragia, *Europolitics. Institutions and Policy-Making in the 'New' EC* (Washington: Brookings Institution).

Matláry, J. H. (1993) 'The Development of Environmental Policy-Making in Hungary: The Role of the EC', CICERO Working Paper, no. 2, Oslo University.

McGowan, F. (1989) 'The Single Energy Market and Energy Policy: Conflicting Agendas?', *Energy Policy*, Dec., pp. 547–53.

McGowan, F. (1993) *The Struggle for Power in Europe: Competition and Regulation in the Electricity Industry* (London: RIIA).

Meerhaege, Michel van (1989) 'The Awkward Difference between Philosophy and Reality', *European Affairs*, vol. 1, pp. 18–23.

Mény, Y. (1990) *Government and Politics in Western Europe: Britain, France, Italy and West Germany* (Oxford: Oxford University Press).

Milward, A. (1992) *The European Rescue of the Nation-State* (Berkeley: University of California Press).

Moravcsik, A. (1991) 'Negotiating the Single European Act: National Interests and Conventional Statecraft in the EC', *International Organization*, vol. 45, no. 1 (Winter).

Moravcsik, A. (1993) 'Preferences and Power in the European Community A Liberal Intergovernmental Approach', *Journal of Common Market Studies*, vol. 31, no. 4.

Moravcsik, A. (1995) 'Liberal Intergovernmentalism and Integration: A rejoinder', *Journal of Common Market Studies*, December, vol. 33, no. 4.

Nelson, B. (1993) *The State Offshore: Petroleum, Politics and State Intervention on the British and Norwegian Continental Shelves* (New York: Praeger).

Norwegian Ministry of Industry and Energy (1994) *Fact Sheet* (Oslo).

Nugent, N. (1994) *The Government and Policies of the European Union* (London: Macmillan).

Padgett, S. (1992) 'The Single European Energy Market: The Politics of Realization', *Journal of Common Market Studies*, vol. xxx, no. 1 (March).

Padoa-Schioppa, T. (1987) *Efficiency, Stability, and Equity* (Oxford: Oxford University Press).

Peters, B. G. (1992) 'Bureaucratic Politics and Institutions of the EU', in A. Sbragia (ed.), *Europolitics* (to follow).

Pierson, P. (1995) 'The Path to European Integration. Historical Institutionalist Analysis', paper, Cambridge, Mass. Harvard Center for European Studies.

Putnam, R. (1988) 'The Logic of Two-Level Games', *International Organization*, vol. 42 (Summer).

Reflection Group's Report (Westendorp Report) Brussels, 5.12.1995.

RIIA (1991) *A Single European Market in Energy*, Conference Report (London: RIIA).

Rittberger, V. and P. Mayer (1993) *Regime Theory and International Relations* (Oxford: Clarendon Press).

Robinson, C. (1982) 'Energy Trends and the Development of Energy Policy in the UK', working paper 61 (University of Surrey, Economics Centre).

Rosenthal, G. (1975) *The Men Behind the Decisions Cases in European Policy-Making* (Lexington, Mass.: D. C. Heath).

Samuels, R. (1987) *The Business of the Japanese State. Energy Markets in Comparative and Historical Perspectives* (Ithaca, NY: Cornell University Press).

Sandholz, W. (1992) *High-Tech Europe. The Politics of International Cooperation* (Berkeley: University of Carolina Press).

Sandholz, W. (1993) 'Choosing Union: Monetary Politics and Maastricht', *International Organization*, 47, Winter.

Sandholz, W. and J. Zysman (1989) '1992: Recasting the European Bargain', *World Politics*, vol. XLII, no. 1 (October).

Sbragia, A. (ed.) *Euro-Politics Institutions and Policy-Making in the 'New' European Community*, Brookings Institution, Washington, DC.

Schmitter, P. C. (1992) 'Interests, Powers, and Functions: Emergent Prospects and Unintended Consequences in the European Policy', unpublished paper (Center for Advanced Study in the Behavioral Sciences).

Schoutheete, P. de (1990) 'The EC and Its Subsystems', in W. Wallace, *The Dynamics of European Integration* (London: Pinter).

Sharp, M. (1990) 'Technology and the Dynamics of Integration, in W. Wallace, *The Dynamics of European Integration* (London: Pinter).

Shonfield, A. (1967) *Modern Capitalism. The Changing Balance of Public and Private Power* (Oxford: Oxford University Press).

Sjöstedt, G. (1977) *The External Role of the European Community* (Farnborough: Gower).

Smith, G. (1978) *Politics in Western Europe* (London: Heinemann Books).

Smouts, M. C. (1977) 'French Foreign Policy: The Domestic Debate', *International Organization*, vol. 53, no. 1.

Stent, A. (1981) *From Embargo to Ostpolitik: The Political Economy of East–West Soviet Relations* (Cambridge: Cambridge University Press).

Stern, J. (1987) *Issues in UK Energy, 1987–92* (London: RIIA).

Stern, J. (1990) *European Gas Markets: Challenge and Opportunity in the 90s* (London: RIIA).

Swann, D. (1989) *The Retreat of the State: Deregulation and Privatization* (London: Wheatsheaf).

Taylor, P. (1983) *The Limits of European Integration* (New York: Columbia University Press).

Toner, G. (1987) 'The IEA and the Development of the Stocks Devision', *Energy Policy*, vol. 5, no. 1 (Feb).

Underdal, A. (1992) 'Arena or Actor? The Role of IGOs in International Environmental Management', working paper (Oslo: CICERO).

Vahl, R. (1992) 'The European Commission's Leading Role: The Conditions for Effectiveness', paper presented at the ECPR's Inaugural Pan-European Conference, Heidelberg, 16–20 September.

Wallace, H. (1990) 'Making Multilateral Negotiations Work', in W. Wallace, *The Dynamics of European Integration* (London: Pinter).

Wallace, W. (1990) 'Introduction', in W. Wallace, *The Dynamics of European Integration* (London: Pinter).

Wallace, W., H. Wallace and C. Webb (1977) *Policy-Making in the European Countries* (London: John Wiley & Sons).

Weber, S. and H. Wiesmith (1991) 'Issue Linkage in the EC', *Journal of Common Market Studies*, vol. XXIX, no. 3 (March).

Wendt, A. (1992) 'Anarchy is What States Make of It: The Social Construction of Power Politics', *International Organization*, vol. 46, no. 2 (Spring).

Wessels, W. (1990) 'Administrative Interaction', in W. Wallace, *The Dynamics of European Integration* (London: Pinter).

Wessels, W. (1991) 'The EC Council: The Country's Decision-Making Centre', in R. Keohane and S. Hoffman, *The New European Community: Decision-Making and Institutional Change* (Boulder: Westview Press).

Wilkinson, D. (1992) *Maastricht and the Environment. The Implications for the EC's Environmental Policy of the Treaty on European Union* (London: Institute for European Environmental Policy).

Wincott, D. (1995) 'Institutional Interaction and European Integration: Towards an Everyday Critique of Liberal Intergovernmentalism', *Journal of Common Market Studies*, vol. 33, no. 4 (December).

Young, O. (1994) *International Governance. Protecting the Enironment in a Stateless Society* (Ithaca, NY: Cornell University Press).

Young, O. and G. Osherenko (1993) *Polar Politics: Creating International Environmental Regimes* (Ithaca, NY: Cornell University Press).

Zysman, J. (1988) *Governments, Markets and Growth: Financial Systems and the Politics of Industrial Change* (Ithaca, NY: Cornell University Press).

EU publications (listed chronologically)

(1983) *The European Community energy options in 1983*, survey prepared by Marie-Martine Buckens (Brussels: European News Agency).

(1985) *White Paper on the Internal Market.*

(1985) *New Community energy objectives.*

(1986) *Quelle politique énergétique pour l'Europe? Propositions pour une relance*, Énergie et société (LXGOSCE) (Grenoble: Institut économique et juridique de l'énergie).

(1987) *Treaties Establishing the EC* (Luxembourg, Office for Official EC Publications).

(1988) *The Internal Energy Market*, Commission Working Document (COM88/238 Final).

(1988) *Proposal for a Council Directive on the Procurement Procedures of Entities Providing Water, Energy and Transport Services* (COM88/337).

(1988) M. M. Buckens, *EEC energy policy and the single market of 1993*, suppl.: The list of obstacles to be overcome to complete the single energy market (Brussels: Prometheus).

(1988) *The list of obstacles to be overcome to complete the single energy market* (COM88/238). An initial European Commission analysis. Suppl. a: EEC energy policy and the single market of 1993 (Brussels: Prometheus).

(1989) *Draft Directive on Transparency of Consumer Energy Prices* (COM89/123).

(1989) *Draft Directive on Natural Gas Transportation* (COM89/334).

(1989) *Draft Directive on Investment Transparency* (COM89/.

(1989) *Energy and the environment.*

(1989) *Proposal for a Council Directive on the transit of electricity through transmission grids* (COM89/336).

(1989) *Draft Council Directive concerning a Community procedure to improve the transparency of gas and electricity prices charged to industrial end-users* (COM 89/.

(1989) *Draft Council Regulation (EEC) amending Regulation (EEC) No 1056/72 on notifying the Commission of investment projects of interest to the Community in the petroleum, natural gas and electricity sectors.*

(1989) *Proposal for a Council Directive on the transit of natural gas through the major systems.*

(1989) *Towards completion of the internal market for natural gas.*

(1990) *Energy in the European Community.* (Luxembourg: Office of EC Publications).

(1990) *PHARE: Assistance á la restructuration économique des pays d'Europe centrale et orientale,* EEC information booklet.

(1990) *The EC and Its Eastern Neighbours,* EC information booklet.

(1990) *The European Investment Bank,* EC information booklet.

(1990) *The Environment and the Internal Market. Challenges and Opportunities.*

(1990) *An Action Programme to Limit Emissions of CO_2 and Improve the Security of Energy Supply.*

(1990) *Communication à la presse,* 1404ième Session of the Council, 21 May 1990.

(1990) *Developing a CO_2 Goal for the Community,* draft communication to the Environmental Council from the Italian Presidency.

(1990) *Climate Change Policy: Conclusions,* declaration from the European Council meeting in Luxembourg.

(1990) *Memorandum pour un point de vue communautaire de l'acton internationale de limitation des émissions de CO_2 d'origine fossile,* French paper to Environmental Council, September.

(1990) *The Environmental Imperative: Declaration by the European Council,* Dublin, June.

(1991) *Proposal for a Council Directive concerning common rules for the internal market in natural gas,* COM91/548.

(1991) *Draft Treaty on the Union,* July.

(1991) *Commission's Work Program.*

(1991) *Draft Communication on the Use of Economic and Fiscal Instruments in EC Environmental Policy,* June, DG XI (later downgraded to 'expert report').

(1991) *Annual report on the Monitoring of the Application of Community Law.*

(1992) *Treaty on Political Union.*

1992 *Presidency's Conclusions,* European Council, Lisbon.

(1992) *Forslag til Rådets Direktiv om betingelser for tildeling og udnyttelse af tilladelser til forundersøgelse, efterforskning og indvinding af kulbrinter (92/110).*

(1994) *Communication on Economic Growth and the Environment* (COM(94)465).

(1994) *Traite de la charte de energie,* Texte a adopter, 14 September 1994.

(1995) *Barcelona declaration.*

EU (1995) *Compendium of Legislation and Other Instruments Relating to Energy,* (Brussels: DGXVII).

(1995) *Green Paper on EU Energy Policy.*

(1995) *EC Gas Supply and Prospects.*

(1996) *White Paper on EU Energy Policy.*

Interviews

The interviews listed below were conducted over several years with politicians, energy press representatives, energy company officials, civil servants in energy ministries and in the EU (Commission, Parliament, national EU representatives) and academics in energy studies. Among those concerned with energy policy, especially when it related to natural gas, there was a great reluctance to be interviewed unless anonymity was agreed to. Thus as a rule I have not quoted the names of any of those interviewed (unless they so agreed) or an affiliation that allows them to be identified.

I did not find it useful to present a standardised questionnaire in the interviews. The topics discussed were however the same: in the national capitals I dealt with the relationship between the state and interest groups in the energy area as well as the stance towards EU energy policy; in the EU I looked for information on the relationship between the four states and EU institutions, and between EU institutions themselves in the policy-making process. The Norwegian embassies in Bonn, Paris, Rome and London were extremely helpful in setting up interviews for me, and they are herewith duly thanked. In Brussels the Norwegian embassy to the EU performed the same role in addition to my own contacts in DGXVII.

Bonn (1985):	Bundestag, party energy spokesmen; Ministry of Economics.
Paris (1985):	Gaz de France, sales manager; *Le Monde*; Commissariat du plan; OECD, IEA: Gas division.
London (1986):	British Gas Corporation; Department of Energy; MPs, House of Commons; MP, House of Lords; Chairman of the Select Committee on Energy.
Rome (1985):	Ministry of Industry.
Brussels (1985, 1986, 1990, 1992):	EU Commission: DG XVII, DG XI, DG IV; environmental NGOs; European Environmental Bureau.
Budapest (1991):	Ministry of the Environment; Head, Academy of Sciences; Director, Regional Environmental Center for Eastern and Central Europe.
Lisbon (1992):	Members of the European Parliament; Member of ECOSOC (Economic and Social Committee); Representatives of DG XVII; Irish, Dutch and French energy policy-makers.

Energy periodicals

Europe: Agence internationale d'information pour la presse, Euro-East, EuropeEnergy, European Energy Report, EC Energy Monthly, International Gas Report, Petroleum Intelligence Weekly, Platt's Oilgram News, Energy in Europe, East European Energy Report, World Gas Report, Norsk Oljerevy, Scan-Energy, Green Energy Matters.

Newspapers

Le Monde, Dagens Næringsliv, Aftenposten, Financial Times.

Index

accords de Luxembourg 143
Alemolo v. Isselmij 122
Andriessen, F. 74, 139

Bayernwerk AG 84
Bohunice 76
British Gas 30
British Gas Corporation 30
Brittan, L. 46, 120
Bundeskartellamt 34, 35, 135
Bundesverfassungsgericht 33

carbon tax 21, 60, 66, 68–70, 78,
   85, 88, 92, 95, 98, 99, 101, 103,
   108–9, 117–18, 125, 127, 157
Cardoso e Cunha, A. 59, 74, 109,
   118, 124
CBI 100
CEDEC 100
CEEP 97, 100
CEFIC 99–100
CEPCED 96, 102
CERT 124–7
Charbonnages de France 36
Charter Conference 76
Charter Secretariat 76
Chernobyl 76–7
CIS 6, 10, 21, 22, 23, 54, 71, 72,
   73–4, 75, 156
CO₂ emissions 9, 31, 41, 67, 69, 70,
   85, 92, 95, 99, 117, 158
coal subsidies 15, 22, 33, 47, 53,
   67, 80–1, 82–3, 86
cohesion funds 51
common carriage 48, 80, 83
common energy policy (CEP) 1, 2,
   7, 9, 10, 13–14, 15, 16, 18, 21,
   23, 24, 35, 51, 58–78, 86, 88–9,

91, 94, 95, 99, 100–1, 102, 103,
   104, 106, 110, 112, 113–16,
   118, 125, 126–7, 129, 137, 138,
   140–1, 152, 153, 154, 155
Compagnie française de
   methane 38
concession policy 56
COREPER 107
Court of First Instance 119
CSCE 75, 91, 109, 139

Delors, J. 61–2, 63, 68, 74, 75, 109,
   139, 144
deregulation 6, 7–8, 10, 19, 28, 30,
   35, 40, 43–4, 45, 47, 53, 57, 88,
   97, 100, 121, 123, 152
Desama. C. 127
Deubner, C. 17

Economic and Social
   Committee 64
ECSC 2, 10, 13, 14, 15–16, 17–18,
   23, 27, 62, 67, 112–13, 127
Électricité de France 36, 38, 50,
   82, 84, 85
Elf Aquitaine 39
emergency oil stocks 18, 101
EMU 4
ENEL 40
energy centres 156
Energy Charter 21, 47, 54, 73, 74,
   78, 88, 100, 103, 109–10, 116,
   133, 138, 140–1, 145, 154, 156
ENI 39, 40, 87
environmental policies 6, 7, 8, 9,
   13, 23, 31, 42, 47, 60, 67, 68, 71,
   77, 91, 108, 117, 118, 125, 138,
   140, 150, 157, 158, 159

ETUC 97, 102
Euratom 2, 3, 10, 13, 14, 16–17,
    18, 23, 27, 62, 77, 127
Eurelectric 96, 98, 101–2, 112
Euro-Mediterranean strategy 54,
    55
Eurogas 52, 96, 100
European Bank for Reconstruction
    and Development 71
European Environmental
    Agency 71
European Environmental
    Bureau 64, 158
European Investment Bank
    (EiB) 52, 71
Europia 96, 99, 101

Faroux, R. 85
Foratom 96, 102

G-7 77
Gaz de France 36, 38, 82, 94
geordneter Markt 32, 35, 44, 46
Green Paper on a CEP 60
Groningen 28
Group of 24 72
Gulf Cooperation Council 69, 157
Gulf War 22, 63, 109, 113–14, 138,
    140

High Authority 15, 18, 24
Hüttenvertrag 33, 80

IFIEC 102
internal energy market (IEM) 2,
    7, 8, 9, 10, 13, 18, 19–23, 24, 35,
    45–57, 58–60, 61, 62, 63, 64, 74,
    77–8, 79, 81, 82, 83, 84, 85–6,
    87–8, 89–90, 91, 93–4, 95, 97–8,
    99, 101, 103, 104, 106, 108, 109,
    110–11, 112–13, 114, 115, 116,
    117, 119, 121, 122, 123, 124,
    126, 127, 128–9, 130–1, 134-8,
    140–1, 145, 151, 152, 153,
    154–5, 159
International Energy Agency 12,
    17, 23, 59, 101, 114

Jahrhundertvertrag 33, 80, 81, 82, 83,
    88, 135

Kissinger, H. 17
Kohl, H. 82, 83, 139
Kohlenpfennig 33, 80, 81, 135
Kozludoy 76
Kronenberger Kreis 80

Lacq 36
Lubbers, R. 73, 116, 138, 139

Maghreb 54–5, 156
Majone, G. 8, 45, 47
Mandil Report 36, 38, 50, 84
Maniatopoulos, C. 139
McKinsey 98
Miert, K. v. 46
Milward, A. 15–16
Mitterrand, F. 19, 82, 83
Monnet, J. 14, 15, 16
Monopolies and Merger
    Commission 30
Monti, M. 157
Moravcsik, A. 5, 141, 144–5

National Power 30
natural monopoly 7, 122

OFFER 30
Ofgas 30, 31
OPEC 17, 26, 69, 99, 101, 157
open access 20, 21, 48, 86, 87, 128,
    131, 160

Padgett, S. 13, 35, 80, 83
Papoutsis, I 155, 159
Pergola, A. 126–7
PHARE 72, 73
plan energetico nazionale 40
PowerGen 30
Preussenelektra AG 84
public procurement 10, 47, 86, 87,
    97
public service function 7, 30, 38,
    40, 54, 98, 120, 122–3, 152, 159
Putnam. R. 3–4, 6, 28, 133, 134,
    136, 137, 146

RECHAR 52–3, 61
Ripa de Meana 118
Ruhrgas 33
RWE Énergie 84

SAVE 158
Schuman Plan 15
SÉA 6, 19, 20, 50, 66, 104, 106,
122
security of supply 6, 7, 8–9, 12,
18, 34, 39, 55, 58–9, 60–1, 62,
63, 77, 86, 100, 102, 114, 120,
123
single buyer (SB) 38, 39, 50, 57,
84, 86, 98, 100, 129
SNAM 87
SO₂ emissions 9
Société Nationale de Gaz du Sud-
Ouest 38
state aid 14, 23, 47, 51, 52–3, 83,
112–13, 120

TACIS 77
Thatcher, Margaret 8, 29, 60, 87
third-party access 21, 48
trans-European networks 21, 51,
52, 62
transparency 10, 16, 20, 47, 56, 63,
86, 87, 93
Treaty on European Union 14, 20,
60, 62, 64, 66, 67, 78, 88, 109,
116, 124, 125, 138, 151, 158
Treaty of Paris 14, 15, 18, 109
'two-level games' 3

unbundling 50
UNCED 23, 69, 118, 119

Verbundnetz Gas 33

Westendorp Report 89
White Paper on Internal
Market 9, 19
World Bank 73, 77